Cooking with F·R·I·E·N·D·S

Cooking with

F·R·I·E·N·D·S

Amy Lyles Wilson with Recipes by Jack Bishop

RUTLEDGE HILL PRESS

Nashville, Tennessee

Published in Nashville, Tennessee, by Rutledge Hill Press, Inc.
211 Seventh Avenue North, Nashville, Tennessee 37219

Distributed in Canada by H.B. Fenn & Company, Ltd.,
1090 Lorimar Drive, Mississauga, Ontario L5S 1R7

Distributed in Australia by Millennium Books,
13/3 Maddox Street, Alexandria NSW 2015

Distributed in New Zealand by Tandem Press, 2 Rugby Road,
Birkenhead, Auckland 10

Distributed in the United Kingdom by Verulam Publishing, Ltd.,
152a Park Street Lane, Park Street, St. Albans, Hertfordshire AL2 2AU

Book design by Bruce Gore / Gore Studio, Inc., Nashville, Tennessee.
Text layout and typesetting by John Wilson and Mark Foltz, Nashville, Tennessee.

Library of Congress Cataloging in Publication Data

Wilson, Amy Lyles, 1961–
    Cooking with Friends / Amy Lyles Wilson; with recipes by Jack Bishop.
       p. cm.
    Includes index.
    ISBN 1-55853-383-4 (hc)
    1. Cookery. 2. Friends (Television program)   I. Bishop, Jack.
  II. Friends (Television program)   III. Title
TX714.W525   1995
    641.5—dc20   95-44066
                                                CIP

Printed in the United States of America
95 96 97 98 99 — 7 6 5 4 3 2
RH1

Contents

Cooking with F·R·I·E·N·D·S

"We have GOT to start locking that door."

Appetizers

**Starting off
with the
right stuff**

Courteney Cox / MONICA

Born and raised in Birmingham, Alabama, Courteney Cox, the youngest of four children, made her comedy television debut on the hit series *Family Ties* as Michael J. Fox's girlfriend, Lauren. In 1994 she appeared in *Ace Ventura: Pet Detective*. In addition, Cox has starred in the television series *The Trouble with Larry* and also guest starred on *Seinfeld, Morton and Hays, Misfits of Science, Murder, She Wrote,* and *Code Name: Fox Fire.* Her feature film credits include *Down Twisted, Masters of the Universe, Cocoon II, Shaking the Tree, Mr. Destiny, Blue Desert, The Opposite Sex,* and *The Philadelphia Experiment II.* Cox's big break came in Bruce Springsteen's 1984 music video "Dancing in the Dark." And yes, she does have at least one thing in common with Monica: In real life she is a neat freak.

Addictive Artichoke Dip

When Janice comes to the gang's New Year's Eve party, she falls for more than Chandler. She can't stay away from "this artichoke thing" made by Monica. "Don't tell me what's in it," whines Janice. But we couldn't resist. It's really quite decadent and requires a total abandonment of self-control. And anyway, according to Janice, "The diet starts tomorrow."

1	**6-ounce jar marinated artichoke hearts, drained**
¼	**cup fresh parsley leaves**
1	**medium clove garlic, peeled**
2	**tablespoons lemon juice**
1½	**cups sour cream**

Salt

Cayenne pepper

▶ Place the artichoke hearts, parsley, garlic, and lemon juice in the work bowl of a food processor or in a blender. Process, scraping down the sides as needed, until the ingredients are finely chopped. Add the sour cream and process until smooth.

▶ Scrape the dip into a serving bowl and stir in salt and cayenne pepper to taste. Cover and refrigerate for at least 1 hour to allow the flavors to blend (or overnight). Serve with crackers or raw vegetables.

Makes about 2 cups, enough for 8

Pepper Jack Crackers

These tiny cheese crackers, made with peppery Monterey Jack, are perfect party food. Serve with a bowl of olives and cocktails for a simple but classy spread.

8   tablespoons (I stick) unsalted butter, softened

½   pound Pepper Jack (Monterey Jack with chilies) or other cheese (such as plain Jack or Cheddar), finely grated

I   cup flour

½   teaspoon salt

▶ Cream the butter with an electric mixer until light and fluffy, about 2 minutes. Beat in the cheese until well mixed. Stir together the flour and salt. Slowly work in the dry ingredients. The dough will be fairly stiff. Roll the dough into two 10-inch-long logs that are about an inch thick. Wrap the logs in plastic and chill them in the freezer for 2 hours.

▶ Preheat the oven to 375°. Working with one log at a time, remove it from the freezer and slice it into ¼-inch-thick rounds. Place the rounds on 2 large ungreased baking sheets. Bake until the crackers are golden, 10 to 12 minutes. Cool the crackers on a rack. They are delicious warm but can be stored in an airtight container for a few days.

Makes about 50 crackers, enough for 8 with drinks

Indian Sweet Potato Chips with Curry

Try as she might, Monica can't slip anything past her mother. (Who can?) As Mrs. Geller (as played by Christina Pickles) samples one of Monica's creations, she asks in a disapproving tone, "What's that curry taste?" The only appropriate response, of course, is "curry." If your guests ask what's that curry flavor, tell them to shut up and eat or go to their rooms.

2   pounds sweet potatoes

2   tablespoons vegetable oil

I   teaspoon curry powder

I   teaspoon salt

▶ Preheat the oven to 450°. Scrub the sweet potatoes under cold, running water, but do not peel them. Slice the potatoes crosswise into ⅛-inch-thick rounds. Place the potatoes in a large bowl. Combine the oil, curry powder, and salt in a small bowl. Drizzle the curry oil over the potatoes and mix well with your hands to ensure that the potato slices are evenly coated with the oil.

▶ Spread the potato slices in a single layer over 2 large baking sheets. Bake the potatoes, turning them once, until crisp, about 15 minutes. Do not let the sweet potatoes burn. Transfer the baked potato chips to a napkin-lined basket. Serve hot from the oven.

Serves 4 to 6 with drinks

Ross:
Carol. Honey. Shh. Everything's gonna be all right.

Carol:
Oh, what do you know? No one's going up to you, saying, "Hi. Is that your nostril? Mind if we push this pot roast through it?!"

Ugly Naked Guy Nacho Chips

Making your own tortilla chips is incredibly easy—even Joey and Chandler could do it—and allows you to add as much (or as little) salt as desired. Serve these naked chips with one of the salsa recipes that follow or top them with your favorite nacho ingredients, such as onions, refried beans, cheese, jalapeños, and cooked meat.

18 **6-inch yellow or blue tortillas (usually found in the refrigerated case at the supermarket)**
Nonstick vegetable oil spray
Salt

▶ Preheat the oven to 350°. Cut the tortillas into 8 wedges. Generously spray 2 large baking sheets with vegetable oil. Spread the tortillas evenly over the sheets, making sure that the pieces do not overlap. Sprinkle with salt to taste.

▶ Bake the tortillas until crisp, 5 to 10 minutes. Cool the tortillas for several minutes on the baking sheets and then transfer them to a serving basket or top as nachos (broil to melt cheese).

Makes 144 tortilla chips, enough for 8 to 10

Chicken Wings with Spicy Mustard Glaze

When *Friends* go out, someone invariably gets an order of chicken wings—or two. For snacking at home, this Asian-style glaze is sweet, spicy, and sour all at once.

⅓ **cup Dijon mustard**
¼ **cup cider vinegar**
¼ **cup orange juice**
½ **cup honey**
¼ **cup soy sauce**
4 **medium cloves garlic, minced**
1 **tablespoon Chinese chile oil**
16 **chicken wings (about 3 pounds)**

▶ Mix the mustard, vinegar, orange juice, honey, soy sauce, garlic, and chile oil in a large bowl. Remove and discard the tips from the chicken wings. Place the wings in the bowl with the mustard mixture. Turn to coat the wings well. Cover and marinate in the refrigerator for at least 30 minutes or up to 4 hours.

▶ Preheat the oven to 400°. Lift the chicken wings from the marinade and place them in a single layer on a large baking sheet. Bake the wings, basting once with the remaining marinade, until they are cooked through, 25 to 30 minutes. Turn the oven to broil. Slide the baking sheet under the broiler and cook just until the skins brown and become crisp, no more than 5 minutes. Serve spicy wings immediately with plenty of beer—and napkins.

Serves 4 to 6

Real South-of-the-Border Tomato Salsa

You can serve salsa from a bottle, but making your own with summer tomatoes is so easy and so much more delicious. Serve with tortilla chips and either Mexican beer or margaritas.

3   large ripe tomatoes, cored and cut into ¼-inch cubes

I   small red onion, minced

2   medium cloves garlic, minced

3   tablespoons minced fresh cilantro leaves

2   tablespoons lime juice

I to 2 small jalapeño peppers, stemmed and minced (you decide how hot!)

   Salt

▶   Place the tomatoes, onion, garlic, cilantro, lime juice, and peppers in a medium bowl. Add salt to taste and mix gently. Serve immediately with tortilla chips or cover and refrigerate for up to 1 day.

Makes about 4 cups, enough for 8 to 10

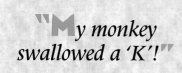

"My monkey swallowed a 'K'!"

> **H O R S   D ' O E U V R E**
>
> **A French word meaning "outside the work." Another term for appetizer.**

Avocado Salsa

You might not think of guacamole as a kind of salsa, but it is. In this version, the ingredients are left fairly chunky. You can mash up the avocado for a smoother texture, but that's more work and the flavor is the same. Pebbly skinned avocados are firmer and creamier than those with smooth skins and should be used here. For a real Mexican fiesta, whip up several kinds of salsa and serve with both blue and yellow corn tortilla chips.

3   medium ripe avocados, peeled, pitted, and cut into ½-inch chunks

2   medium plum tomatoes, cored and cut into ¼-inch cubes

2   medium cloves garlic, minced

2   scallions, white and light green parts sliced thin

2   tablespoons lemon juice

I   tablespoon minced fresh oregano or cilantro leaves

   Salt

   Bottled hot sauce (such as Tabasco)

▶   Place the avocados, tomatoes, garlic, scallions, lemon juice, and oregano in a medium bowl. Add salt and hot sauce to taste and mix gently. Serve immediately (the avocado will turn brown fairly quickly) with tortilla chips.

Makes 3 cups, enough for 8 to 10

Rachel:
I'm being a total laundry spaz? Am I supposed to use, like, one machine for shirts, and another machine for pants?

Ross:
Have you never done this before?

Rachel:
Well, not myself. But I know other people that have. Okay, you caught me. I'm a laundry virgin.

Mango and Black Bean Salsa

This tropical salsa is bursting with flavor and contains no oil at all. Scoop up this chunky mixture with tortilla chips and serve with plenty of ice-cold beer.

3	**medium mangoes, peeled, pitted, and cut into ¼-inch cubes**
1	**15-ounce can black beans, drained and rinsed**
1	**small red onion, diced**
3	**tablespoons minced fresh cilantro leaves**
3	**tablespoons lime juice**
1	**teaspoon ground cumin**
1	**medium serrano or jalapeño pepper, stemmed and minced**
	Salt

▶ Place the mango cubes, black beans, onion, cilantro, lime juice, cumin, and serrano or jalapeño in a medium bowl. Add salt to taste and mix gently. Serve immediately with tortilla chips or cover and refrigerate for up to 1 day.

Makes about 4 cups, enough for 8 to 10

"Hello! *Were we at the same table? It's like ... it's like ... cocktails in Appalachia!* **"**

Goat Cheese Canapés

Goat cheese is combined with cream and then spread over toasted rounds of Italian bread that have been rubbed with garlic. A sprinkling of fresh herbs completes this easy-to-prepare appetizer.

8	**ounces fresh goat cheese**
1	**long loaf Italian bread, sliced into ½-inch-thick rounds**
1	**large clove garlic, peeled**
2	**tablespoons heavy cream**
	Minced fresh basil, parsley, or chives

▶ Remove the goat cheese from the refrigerator, place it in a medium bowl, and let it warm to room temperature. While you are waiting for the goat cheese to warm up, preheat the broiler. Place the rounds of Italian bread on a large baking sheet. Toast the bread, turning once, until golden on both sides. Rub the top of the slices with the garlic and set them aside.

▶ Use a spatula or heavy spoon to work the cream into the goat cheese. Spread the goat cheese mixture over the garlic-rubbed toasts. Garnish each toast with a sprinkling of minced fresh herbs. Serve fairly soon (within an hour) or toasts will get soggy, especially on a muggy summer night.

Makes about 24 canapés, enough for 8

Bacchus Basics

Although choosing a wine can be a daunting task, it needn't be. Like anything else, it will be easier when you know the score.

- Do your homework. Ask someone at your local wine store to help you. People who sell wine for a living should know their products. Those who do like to talk about them. Check to see if any of the stores in your area offer tastings or seminars, which are common in many cities. Read related magazines and newspaper columns. The food editor at your local paper might be able to recommend some sources for you.

- Compare prices. Don't assume that price reflects quality. There are a lot of good, moderately priced ($10–$15) wines out there. On the flip side, don't immediately snap up bottles that have been marked down. It may be that those wines are about to turn to vinegar. And even though a lot of stores would let you return the bad bottle, who wants the hassle?

- Tilt it. Don't store your wine bottles standing upright. Doing so may dry out the corks, thereby allowing air to enter the bottles and change the flavor.

- Chill out. Take white wines out of the refrigerator twenty minutes before serving, and put red wines (not all reds need refrigeration) in twenty minutes before you plan to pop the cork.

- Take note. If you drink something you like, whether at home, in a restaurant, or at a friend's house, jot down the name and year. Just like videos and books, you'll forget which one you wanted the next time you go to the store.

- Trust your taste buds. Let your preferences and your mood be your guide. When in doubt, go with the tried and true: Cabernet Sauvignon with steak, Chardonnay with chicken, and Sauvignon Blanc with fish.

Monica:
*Okay. Try this salmon
mousse.*

Joey:
Mmm. Good.

Monica:
*Is it better than the other
salmon mousse?*

Joey:
It's . . . creamier.

Monica:
Yeah, but is that better?

Joey:
*I don't know. We're
talking about whipped
fish, Monica. I'm just
happy I'm keeping it
down, you know?*

"Whipped Fish" on Endive

Despite Joey's half-hearted
endorsement of merely "keeping it
down," this creamy mousse is
delicious, especially when served on
endive leaves.

I	**envelope unflavored gelatin**
¼	**cup cold water**
½	**cup boiling water**
½	**cup sour cream**
2	**tablespoons minced fresh dill leaves**
I	**teaspoon salt**
½	**teaspoon paprika**
2	**cups finely flaked canned or cooked salmon (poach your own fish if you like)**
I	**cup heavy cream**
4	**large heads Belgian endive**

► Sprinkle the gelatin over the cold
water in a large bowl. Let stand
for 2 minutes. Whisk in the
boiling water until the gelatin
dissolves. Cool to room temperature
while you gather and prepare the
remaining ingredients.

► Whisk in the sour cream, dill, salt,
and paprika until smooth. Refrigerate until the mixture starts to
thicken up, about 20 minutes or
so. Get the salmon ready, and
whip the cream with an electric
mixer while you are waiting for
the sour cream mixture to
thicken.

► Carefully separate the long endive
leaves, being sure not to break
them. Wash and dry the endive
and arrange the leaves on a
serving platter. Fold the flaked
salmon into the thickened sour
cream mixture. Gently fold in the
whipped cream.

► Monica would probably use a
pastry bag to pipe the mousse
onto the endive leaves, but you
can use a spoon to dollop a little
mousse onto each endive leaf. You
won't be able to make fancy
shapes this way, but the mousse
will look and taste fine. Chill the
endive for up to 2 hours.

Serves 12 to 15 at an elegant cocktail party

Smoked Salmon Canapés with Dill Cream Cheese

Smoked salmon is cheaper than you
think, especially when portioned out
over so many little pumpernickel
toasts.

I	**square loaf pumpernickel bread, sliced**
8	**ounces cream cheese, at room temperature**
2	**tablespoons minced fresh dill leaves, plus more for garnish**
2	**tablespoons lemon juice**
½	**teaspoon ground black pepper**
½	**pound thinly sliced smoked salmon, slices cut in half**

► Preheat the broiler. Cut the slices
of pumpernickel bread on the
diagonal into 4 triangles. Toast the
triangles under the broiler until
crisp. Beat the cream cheese, dill,
lemon juice, and pepper with an
electric mixer or heavy spoon
until well combined.

► Spread some of the dill cream
cheese over each toast. Lay a piece
of salmon over each toast and
garnish with a tiny piece of dill.
Serve promptly or chill for up to 2
hours.

Makes about 60 canapés, enough for 15

Chicken Brochettes with Peanut Dipping Sauce

This substantial appetizer takes its cues from satés. Here the skewered chicken pieces are cooked on top of the stove, making this a year-round, apartment-friendly recipe.

1½	**pounds boneless, skinless chicken breasts**
3	**tablespoons soy sauce**
2	**medium cloves garlic, minced**
1	**tablespoon dark sesame oil**
1	**tablespoon lemon juice**
2	**medium scallions, white and light green parts sliced thin**
3	**tablespoons finely chopped unsalted peanuts**
2	**tablespoons vegetable oil**

▶ Trim any excess fat from the chicken and cut the meat into 1½-inch pieces. Toss the chicken with 1 tablespoon soy sauce and the garlic and marinate for 10 minutes while you prepare the dipping sauce.

▶ Combine the remaining 2 tablespoons soy sauce with the sesame oil, lemon juice, scallions, and peanuts. Set the sauce aside in a small serving bowl.

▶ Thread the chicken pieces on twelve 4- or 5-inch-long wooden toothpicks or skewers. Heat the vegetable oil in a large nonstick skillet. Add the chicken and cook (in batches if necessary) until nicely browned on both sides, about 5 minutes total. Place the skewered chicken on a platter and pass with the peanut dipping sauce. Serve hot.

Makes 12 skewers, enough for 6 as an appetizer

Spiced Pecans

These party nuts are habit forming. Serve with drinks to get things off to a fiery start.

1	**tablespoon chili powder**
1	**tablespoon paprika**
1	**teaspoon ground cumin**
½	**teaspoon cayenne pepper**
½	**teaspoon ground ginger**
2	**teaspoons salt**
6	**cups pecan halves**
¼	**cup vegetable oil**

▶ Preheat the oven to 325°. Combine the spices and salt in a small bowl. Toss the pecans and oil in a large bowl. Sprinkle the spice mixture over the nuts and mix well. Spread the nuts out in a single layer over 2 large baking sheets. Toast until the nuts are fragrant, about 10 minutes. Cool the nuts to room temperature. (The nuts can be stored in an airtight container for several days.) Serve a little at a time, or otherwise you'll find your guests have devoured all of the nuts in just minutes.

Makes 6 cups, enough for 15 to 20

❦ SATÉ ❧
A dish of southeast Asia consisting of strips of marinated meat, poultry, or seafood, usually grilled on skewers and dipped in peanut sauce.

Chandler:
I can't believe you would actually say that. I would much rather be Mr. Peanut than Mr. Salty.

Joey:
No way. Mr. Salty is a sailor. He's gotta be, like, the toughest snack there is.

Ross:
I don't know. You don't want to mess with Corn Nuts. They're craaazy.

Joey:
All right. I'll give you this: Mr. Peanut is a better dresser. He's got the monocle, he's got the top hat. . . .

Phoebe:
You know he's gay.

Ross:
I just want to clarify this. Are you "outing" Mr. Peanut?

Dr. Rosen:
This hummus is great.

Dr. Mitchell:
God bless the chickpea.

—⁂—

Rachel:
Aren't you a little cute to be a doctor?

—⁂—

Dr. Rosen:
Here. We brought wine.

Dr. Mitchell:
And look: It's from the cellars of Ernest and Tova Borgnine. How could we resist?

Hummus for Doctors and Other Dates

When those cute *ER* doctors visit the apartment, the evening heads downhill as Monica and Rachel, who have switched roles to continue their insurance charade, criticize each other. "Did I mention that I think I'm cuter than I am?" quips Monica. "By the way, in high school, I was a cow," comes Rachel's response. This Middle Eastern dip, no matter how delicious, simply could not resuscitate the date.

1	19-ounce can chickpeas, rinsed and drained
1	medium clove garlic, peeled
¼	cup lemon juice
2	tablespoons olive oil
¼	cup tahini (sesame paste)
⅓	cup plain yogurt
½	teaspoon ground cumin
	Salt
2	tablespoons minced fresh parsley leaves for garnish
	Pita chips, crackers, and/or raw vegetables

▶ Place the chickpeas and garlic in the work bowl of a food processor or in a blender. Process, scraping down the sides as needed, until the ingredients are finely chopped. Add the lemon juice, oil, tahini, yogurt, and cumin and process until smooth. Scrape the hummus into a serving bowl and stir in salt to taste. Garnish bowl with parsley. Serve with toasted pita chips, crackers, or raw vegetables.

▶ And remember, if you're on a double date, don't criticize each other in front of the dates.

Makes about 3 cups, enough for 8

Roasted Bar Nuts with Rosemary

These spicy, rosemary-scented nuts are an adaptation of a recipe served at the bar at the Union Square Cafe, one of New York's top restaurants. Whip up a batch for an after-work cocktail party or just to munch on while watching TV. You can add other unsalted nuts.

1	cup unsalted dry-roasted peanuts
1	cup shelled walnut or pecan pieces
1	cup whole unpeeled almonds
½	cup unsalted cashews
1	tablespoon olive oil
1	tablespoon minced fresh rosemary leaves
1	tablespoon brown sugar
½	teaspoon chili powder
1	teaspoon salt

▶ Preheat the oven to 350°. Spread the nuts out in a single layer on a large baking sheet. Toast the nuts in the oven until they become fragrant, about 7 minutes. Do not let the nuts burn. (Toasting nuts makes them especially delicious, but charring them is a disaster.)

▶ While the nuts are roasting, combine the oil, rosemary, brown sugar, chili powder, and salt in a medium bowl. Add the hot nuts and toss gently. Cool slightly. Transfer nuts to a fancy serving bowl (a glass dish looks great). Serve warm.

Makes about 3½ cups, enough for 8 with drinks

Broiled Oysters with Parsley Pesto

When Joey abandons Chandler at that fancy restaurant, he also leaves behind his credit card. Chandler and Janice run up quite a bill, ordering the best champagne in the house. This fancy oyster hors d'oeuvre is a must with sparkling wine. Eat as many oysters as you like, but go easy on the bubbly, or risk waking up the next morning with your very own date from hell.

I	cup fresh parsley leaves
2	small cloves garlic, peeled
I	tablespoon pine nuts or walnuts
2	tablespoons lemon juice
¼	cup olive oil
½	teaspoon salt
¼	teaspoon ground black pepper
36	shucked oysters on the shell
3	tablespoons plain bread crumbs
	Lemon wedges

► Place the parsley, garlic, nuts, and lemon juice in the work bowl of a food processor or in a blender. Process, scraping down the sides as needed, until the ingredients are finely chopped. With the motor running, slowly pour the oil through the feed tube (or into the blender) and process until smooth. Scrape the sauce into a small bowl. Stir in the salt and pepper.

► Preheat the broiler. Place the shucked oysters in their shells on a large baking sheet. Dollop each with ¾ teaspoon parsley pesto. Lightly sprinkle each oyster with bread crumbs. Broil until the bread crumbs are golden, about 4 minutes. Serve hot with lemon wedges on the side.

Serves 6

Marinated Spanish Olives with Garlic and Herbs

This tapa is great at parties or for snacking while watching *Jeopardy* in Spanish when your monkey's got the remote—again.

½	pound mixed olives with pits (use both green and black olives in a variety of sizes)
¼	cup olive oil
2	large cloves garlic, sliced thin
	Sprigs of fresh thyme, rosemary, or oregano
½	small lemon
	Ground black pepper

► Combine the olives, oil, garlic, and herbs in a small glass jar or plastic container with a lid. Use a vegetable peeler or zester to remove the yellow skin from the lemon half. If removed with a peeler, slice the zest into very thin strips. Add the lemon zest and pepper to taste to the olive mixture. Stir gently. Marinate at room temperature for at least 4 hours or as long as 1 day.

► When ready to serve, simply put out the glass jar and let the party guests help themselves. If the olives were marinated in a plastic container, pour them into a bowl. Marinated olives are great with drinks, especially wine or sangria.

Makes about 1 cup, enough for 6 to 8

Monica:
It's supposed to be that small. It's a pre-appetizer. The French call it an amuse bouche.

Chandler:
Well, it is "amoozing."

Rachel:
Cool. "Urkel" in Spanish is "Urkel."

Cherry Tomatoes Marinated in Pepper Vodka

Tiny cherry tomatoes are perfect party food. Soaking them in a spicy pepper vodka dresses them up nicely. The technique is much like that used to soak a watermelon with vodka, only classier. Place the tomatoes and some of the marinating liquid in a serving bowl and let guests skewer tomatoes with toothpicks or use their fingers.

1   **pint ripe cherry tomatoes**
⅔   **cup pepper vodka**
2   **tablespoons kosher or coarse salt**
1   **tablespoon minced fresh thyme leaves**

▶ Carefully skewer each cherry tomato in a half dozen places with a toothpick. (This lets the vodka penetrate and flavor the tomatoes.) Place the tomatoes in a bowl and add the vodka. Marinate the tomatoes, turning them occasionally, for several hours.

▶ Combine the salt and thyme and place the mixture in a small bowl. Drain off most of the vodka. (You might want to reserve the vodka for making Bloody Marys; it already has a faint tomato flavor.) Place the tomatoes and a little of the vodka in a serving bowl. Let guests skewer tomatoes with toothpicks and then dip them into the seasoned herb salt.

Makes 2 cups, enough for 6

Out West White Bean Dip

The chili powder, cumin, cilantro, and lime juice give this spicy dip its southwestern character, and, hence the name. Urban dwellers as well as ranch hands will appreciate these bold flavors, especially when scooped up on toasted pitas or other crisp crackers.

1   **19-ounce can cannellini beans, drained and rinsed**
2   **medium cloves garlic, peeled**
¼   **cup fresh cilantro leaves**
¼   **cup olive oil**
2   **tablespoons lime juice**
2   **teaspoons chili powder**
1   **teaspoon ground cumin**
    Salt
    Pita crisps or other crackers and assorted raw vegetables

▶ Place the beans, garlic, and cilantro leaves in the work bowl of a food processor or in a blender. Process, scraping down the sides as needed, until the ingredients are finely chopped. Add the oil, lime juice, chili powder, and cumin and process until smooth. Scrape the dip into a serving bowl. Stir in salt to taste. The dip can be covered and refrigerated overnight or eaten right away. Serve with plenty of crackers and maybe some raw vegetables.

Makes about 2 cups, enough for 6 to 8

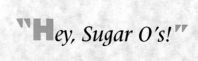

Monica:

It's so great. He showed me where the restaurant's gonna be. It's this cute little place on Tenth Street. It's not too big, it's not too small . . . it's just right.

Chandler:

Was it formerly owned by a blonde woman and some bears?

Monica:

So, anyway, I'm cooking dinner for him Monday night. You know, kind of like an audition. And Phoebe, he really wants you to be here, which would be great for me, 'cause then you could "ooh" and "aah" and make yummy noises.

Rachel:

What are you going to make?

Phoebe:

Yummy noises. I—

Rachel:

And, Monica, what are you going to make?

Monica:

I don't know. It's got to be so great. . . .

Phoebe:

Oh! I know what you can make. I know. Oh, you should make that thing, you know, with the stuff. You know that thing, with the stuff? Okay, I don't know.

Onion Tartlets à la Monica

Monica served this fancy appetizer when she invited a restaurant owner (as played by Jon Lovitz) over to sample some of her cooking. Although the tryout was a disaster, it wasn't because of these delicious little tarts.

Pastry

1⅓	**cups flour**
½	**teaspoon salt**
8	**tablespoons (1 stick) chilled unsalted butter, cut into small pieces**
3 to 4	**tablespoons cold water**

Filling

2	**tablespoons olive oil**
4	**medium onions, sliced thin**
1	**tablespoon sugar**
	Salt and ground black pepper
2	**large eggs**
¾	**cup milk**

▶ Place the flour and salt in the work bowl of a food processor. Add the butter and pulse until the mixture resembles coarse crumbs. Add the cold water 1 tablespoon at a time and pulse just until the dough comes together. Turn the dough out onto a floured counter and roll it to a thickness of ⅛ inch. Use a 3½-inch round cookie cutter or juice glass to punch out about 18 circles of dough.

▶ Grease 2 regular 12-cup muffin tins. Press each circle into 1 cup, gently pushing the dough part way up the side of each cup. (There will be some empty cups.) Chill the pastry in the muffin tins while you prepare the filling.

▶ Heat the oil in a large nonstick skillet. Add the onions and cook over medium heat, stirring occasionally, until they are soft and you are no longer crying, about 10 minutes. Stir in the sugar and continue cooking until the onions turn a rich golden brown, 5 to 10 minutes. Lower the heat if the onions start to burn at any time. Season the caramelized onions with salt and pepper to taste and set them aside.

▶ Preheat the oven to 400°. Divide the onion mixture among the pastry shells. Beat the eggs with a fork in a measuring cup. Beat in the milk. Carefully pour a tablespoon or so of the egg mixture into each pastry shell. Bake until the edges of the pastry turn golden brown and the filling is set, about 20 minutes.

▶ Unmold tartlets by running a sharp knife around their edges and turning them gently out onto a kitchen towel. Serve the tartlets warm with champagne or fancy cocktails. This is not beer food!

Makes 18 tartlets, enough for 6 with drinks

*"*H*ey, Sugar O's!"*

Central Perks

Coffee,
coffee drinks,
muffins,
and such

Ross:
I just thought we'd go out to dinner. And then I'd bring her back to my place and I'd introduce her to my monkey.

Chandler:
And he's not speaking metaphorically.

Orange Shortbread

These thin, buttery bars are a breeze to make. Bake them at a low oven temperature to prevent the shortbread from browning.

8	**tablespoons (1 stick) unsalted butter, softened**
½	**cup confectioners' sugar**
1	**medium orange**
½	**teaspoon vanilla extract**
1	**cup flour**
¼	**teaspoon salt**

▶ Preheat the oven to 300°. Grease an 8-inch-square baking pan and set it aside.

▶ Cream the butter and sugar with an electric mixer until light and fluffy, about 1 minute. Grate the orange zest from the skin of the orange, leaving behind the bitter white pith. When you have 1 teaspoon of grated zest, halve the orange and squeeze out the juice. Add the zest and 2 tablespoons fresh orange juice to the batter along with the vanilla, flour, and salt. Mix until just combined.

▶ Press the dough into the prepared pan with your fingers. Bake until the shortbread is pale gold in color, 30 to 35 minutes. Cool the pan on a rack for 15 minutes and then cut the shortbread into bars.

Makes 16 small bars

"You guys wanna get some coffee?"

Blueberry Muffins

Mornings mean muffins, and none are finer than these, bursting with blueberries.

2	**cups flour**
1	**teaspoon baking soda**
1	**teaspoon grated lemon zest**
16	**tablespoons (2 sticks) unsalted butter, melted**
1	**cup sugar**
2	**large eggs**
½	**cup sour cream**
1	**cup blueberries**

▶ Preheat the oven to 375°. Grease a regular 12-cup muffin tin and set it aside.

▶ Stir together the flour, baking soda, and lemon zest in a medium bowl and set it aside.

▶ Combine the melted butter, sugar, and eggs in a large bowl. Stir in the sour cream. Stir in all but 1 tablespoon of the flour mixture. Place the blueberries in the bowl with the remaining flour mixture and toss gently. Fold the flour-dusted blueberries into the batter.

▶ Spoon the batter into the prepared muffin tin, filling the cups almost to the brim. Bake until the muffins are golden brown and a toothpick inserted in the center comes out clean, 20 to 25 minutes. Cool the muffins in the tin for 5 minutes, turn them out onto a rack, and eat them as soon as you can. There's no better way to start the day than with a warm blueberry muffin and a cup of good coffee.

Makes 12 muffins

CP Caffè Latte

A perennial favorite at Central Perk and coffee houses across the country. The proportions can be doubled.

1½	**ounces brewed espresso**
	Sugar
6	**ounces cold milk**
	Ground cinnamon or cocoa, optional

▶ Prepare a single espresso and pour it into a warmed 10-ounce bowl-shaped cup or tall 10-ounce glass. Stir in sugar to taste. Pour the milk into a small metal pitcher and steam until hot. Do not let milk become frothy or foamy. Pour the steamed milk into the cup with the espresso. Sprinkle with cinnamon or cocoa, if desired, and serve immediately.

Serves 1

❦ LATTE ❦

A cappuccino with just steamed milk and no foam or froth.

Roger:
Actually, it's quite, you know, typical behavior when you have this kind of dysfunctional group dynamic. You know, this sort of co-dependent, emotionally stunted, sitting in your stupid coffee house, with your stupid big cups—which, I'm sorry, might as well have nipples on them. And you're all like: "I need love! I need love! Define me! Define me! Love me! I need love!"

Joey's Walnut Scones

While hanging out at Central Perk one day, Joey gets hit on the head with this English baked good after he makes a rather forward comment about a woman. (What else is new?) "Thanks," he says, clueless, as he begins to munch. Instead of tossing these at loved ones, serve your scones with butter or jam, or eat them plain with a big bowl of latte.

Chandler:
What? Is it 'cause she left you? Is it 'cause she's a lesbian? Is it 'cause she left you for another woman who likes women?

Ross:
A little louder, okay? I think there's a man on the twelfth floor in a coma who didn't quite hear you.

2 ¼	**cups flour**
1 ½	**teaspoons baking powder**
½	**teaspoon salt**
⅓	**cup sugar**
6	**tablespoons cold unsalted butter, cut into pieces**
1	**cup milk**
½	**cup chopped walnuts**

► Preheat the oven to 425°. Grease a large baking sheet and set it aside.

► Place the flour, baking powder, salt, and sugar in the work bowl of a food processor and pulse to combine the ingredients. Add the butter and pulse until the mixture resembles coarse crumbs. Slowly pour the milk through the feed tube and pulse until the dough just comes together.

► Turn the dough out onto a floured counter and knead in more flour if it seems overly sticky. Knead in the nuts by hand. Roll the dough into a 9-inch square that is about ½ inch thick. Cut the dough into nine 3-inch squares.

► Place the squares on the prepared baking sheet, leaving 2 inches between each piece of dough. Bake until the scones are golden brown, about 12 to 15 minutes. Serve immediately.

Makes 9 scones

Double Coffee Milkshake

Take a regular coffee milkshake and add some espresso for a coffee house treat with a real jolt. Although this shake looks like a kid's drink, the flavors are for adults only. To double the recipe, make twice as much espresso, but prepare each shake individually in the blender unless you want ice cream on the ceiling.

¼	**cup brewed espresso or strong coffee, cooled**
½	**cup milk**
2	**scoops coffee ice cream**

► Place the espresso, milk, and ice cream in a blender. Choose the highest setting (frappé always sounds good, so use that one if possible) and blend until smooth. Pour the shake into a tall glass, add a straw, and begin slurping pronto.

Makes 1 large shake

E S P R E S S O

A strong coffee brewed by forcing steam under pressure through darkly roasted, powdered coffee beans.

Marcel's Banana Bread

When Marcel gets kidnapped by nasty Mr. Heckles, Ross and Rachel track him down by following a case of bananas. If you have more bananas than you can eat—and no monkey on hand—turn them into this sweet loaf loaded with nuts.

6	tablespoons (¾ stick) unsalted butter, softened
½	cup sugar
2	large eggs
½	teaspoon vanilla extract
1½	cups mashed bananas (about 3 medium)
1½	cups flour
2	teaspoons baking powder
½	teaspoon salt
¾	cup chopped walnuts

▶ Preheat the oven to 350°. Grease a 9x5-inch loaf pan and set it aside.

▶ Cream the butter and sugar with an electric mixer until light and fluffy, about 1 minute. Beat in the eggs and vanilla until smooth. Stir in the mashed bananas.

▶ Stir together the flour, baking powder, and salt in a small bowl. Fold the dry ingredients into the batter until just blended. Stir in the nuts.

▶ Scrape the batter into the prepared pan. Bake until the banana bread is nicely browned and a toothpick inserted in the center comes out clean, about 1 hour. Cool the pan on a rack for 5 minutes before gently turning the banana bread onto the rack.

Continue cooling to room temperature before slicing.

Serves 6 to 8

Quick-Fix Granola

Even when you're far from the trail, this crunchy granola is the best mix for munching in the morning. Add a latte and a glass of fresh orange juice for a complete breakfast.

2	cups old-fashioned rolled oats
1	teaspoon ground cinnamon
½	cup sliced raw almonds
¼	cup vegetable oil
2	tablespoons honey
1	teaspoon vanilla extract
½	cup raisins or other dried fruit

▶ Preheat the oven to 325°. Grease a large baking sheet and set it aside.

▶ Mix the oats, cinnamon, almonds, oil, honey, and vanilla in a large bowl. (You can add other nuts if you like.)

▶ Spread the granola over the prepared baking sheet. Bake, turning twice, until the granola is golden brown, about 15 minutes. Do not let the granola burn. (Blackened oats are not some new Cajun-style breakfast treat.)

▶ Pour the toasted granola into a large container and stir in the raisins. When cooled, cover the container (granola will keep at room temperature for several weeks) or start eating the granola right away.

Serves 4

Monica:
Get up. Come on. Let's get some coffee.

Chandler:
Oh, okay. 'Cause we never do that.

Joey:
Well, given that he's desperately in love with you, he probably wouldn't mind getting a cup of coffee or something.

Chandler:

Hey, listen, I know I came in late last week, but I slept funny and my hair was. . . .

Banana-Bran Muffins

These muffins are perfect for breakfast on the run. Make a batch on the weekend and freeze them for later. To defrost, wrap individual muffins in foil and place in a 400° oven just as you jump into the shower on Monday morning. By the time you're out of the shower (about 15 minutes), the muffins should be ready. Eat one while you work on your hair. (If you're anything like Chandler, you might need two.)

1½ **cups shredded bran cereal (such as All-Bran)**
1¼ **cups buttermilk**
2 **small ripe bananas, peeled and mashed**
2 **tablespoons vegetable oil**
¼ **cup honey**
¼ **cup firmly packed brown sugar**
1 **large egg**
1½ **cups flour (use part whole-wheat flour, if you want to feel especially healthy)**
2 **teaspoons baking powder**
1½ **teaspoons baking soda**
¼ **teaspoon salt**
¾ **cup raisins or chopped dried fruit**

▶ Preheat the oven to 400°. Grease a regular 12-cup muffin tin and set it aside.

▶ Combine the bran cereal and buttermilk in a bowl and let stand until the cereal becomes very soft, about 5 minutes.

▶ While the cereal is soaking, beat the bananas, oil, honey, and sugar with an electric mixer until smooth. Beat in the egg and then the cereal mixture.

▶ Stir the flour, baking powder, baking soda, and salt together in

"**W**hy does my cinnamon stick have an eraser?"

a separate bowl. Stir the dry ingredients into the batter. Do not overmix. (Beating only makes muffins tough.) Fold in the raisins.

▶ Spoon the batter into the prepared muffin tin, filling the cups to the brim. Bake until the muffins begin to brown around the edges and a toothpick inserted in the center comes out clean, 20 to 25 minutes. Cool the muffins in the tin for 5 minutes, turn them out onto a rack, and continue to cool them or eat warm.

Makes 12 muffins

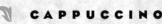

CAPPUCCINO

Espresso coffee mixed or topped with steamed milk. Italian, from resemblance to color of a monk's habit.

Jamie and Fran's Chocolate Biscotti

When the women from *Mad About You* walk into Central Perk, they mistake Phoebe for Ursula and think she's working a second job. They tell Phoebe they want two lattes and some biscotti. Phoebe says "good choice" and sits down. Eventually, Jamie and Fran find a real waiter and get some of these biscotti with macadamia nuts.

2	**cups flour**
½	**cup unsweetened cocoa**
1	**teaspoon baking soda**
¼	**teaspoon salt**
6	**tablespoons (¾ stick) unsalted butter, softened**
1	**cup sugar**
2	**large eggs**
1	**teaspoon vanilla extract**
1	**cup macadamia nuts (can substitute walnuts or pecans)**

▶ Preheat the oven to 350°. Grease and then flour a large baking sheet and set it aside.

▶ Stir the flour, cocoa, baking soda, and salt together in a medium bowl. Set the dry ingredients aside. Cream the butter and sugar with an electric mixer until light and fluffy, about 1 minute. Beat in the eggs and vanilla until smooth. Stir in the dry ingredients until well combined. (The dough will be stiff and fairly dry.) Stir in the nuts.

▶ Turn the dough out onto a floured counter. Divide the dough in half and roll each half into a log that measures about 12 inches

long and 2 inches wide. Transfer the logs to the prepared baking sheet, leaving at least 2 inches between the logs.

▶ Bake the logs until firm to the touch, about 35 minutes. Remove the baking sheet from the oven. Wearing an oven mitt or other protective gear to hold the logs in place, use a serrated knife to cut them crosswise on the diagonal into ¾-inch-thick cookies.

▶ Lay the cookies on one side and return the baking sheet to the oven. Toast until the biscotti are crisp, 5 to 10 minutes. Cool the biscotti on racks and store in an airtight container for weeks. (Chances are they won't last that long.)

Makes 28 long biscotti

Fran:
Look, you're cold, I have to pee, and there's a coffee cup on the window. How bad could it be?

Jamie:
This could be God's way of telling us "eat at home."

Rachel:
I'm not just waitressing. I . . . I . . . also write the specials on the specials board and . . . and I take the dead flowers out of the vase . . . and sometimes Arturo lets me put the chocolate blobbies on the cookies.

Rachel's Peanut Butter Cookies

Rachel is a key member of the Central Perk staff. Why she's even learned to make coffee, write specials on the board, and take dead flowers out of vases. Sometimes, if she's good, the boss even lets her help with these yummy peanut butter cookies.

8	tablespoons (1 stick) unsalted butter, softened
½	cup chunky peanut butter
¾	cup firmly packed brown sugar
¼	cup granulated sugar
1	large egg
1	teaspoon vanilla extract
1⅓	cups flour
½	teaspoon baking powder
½	teaspoon baking soda
36	milk chocolate kisses

▶ Preheat the oven to 375°. Cream the butter and peanut butter with an electric mixer until light and fluffy, about 1 minute. Beat in the sugars until well combined. Beat in the egg and vanilla until smooth.

▶ Stir the flour, baking powder, and baking soda together in a small bowl. Add the dry ingredients to the batter and beat on low until just combined.

▶ Shape the dough into 1-inch balls and place them on 2 large ungreased baking sheets, leaving 2 inches between the balls of dough. Bake until the edges of the cookies are set and just beginning to brown, about 10 minutes. Remove the baking sheets from the oven. Immediately press one chocolate kiss into the center of each cookie. Transfer the cookies to a rack to cool.

Makes 36 cookies

Iced Mocha Latte

This chocolaty espresso drink is the beverage of choice on a hot summer day in the city. Double the proportions if you're cooling off in pairs.

1 to 2 tablespoons chocolate syrup (real chocoholics will want 2)	
1½	ounces brewed espresso
	Sugar
	Ice cubes
6	ounces very cold milk
	Whipped cream (a must if it's really hot out)
	Grated bittersweet or semisweet chocolate for sprinkling on top

▶ Spoon the chocolate syrup into the bottom of a tall 10-ounce glass. Prepare a single espresso and pour it into the glass. Stir in sugar to taste. Chill espresso mixture in the freezer for 15 minutes or add 2 ice cubes. (The ice will dilute the espresso a little, but it does chill the espresso down in seconds.) Stir in the cold milk and add more ice cubes. Dollop with whipped cream and sprinkle with grated chocolate. This coffee drink calls out for a straw and a spoon.

Serves 1

Coffee Talk

More than one writer—and coffee connoisseur—has called coffee the wine of the nineties. And it's no wonder. With thousands of coffee houses possible across America by the year 2000, you need to know what's brewing.

Beans really do make a difference. Arabica beans are richly flavored and grown at high altitudes. Robusta beans, commonly found in supermarket blends, are grown at lower altitudes and yield a flat flavor. Dark roast beans are great for espresso. Medium roast will have more subtle flavors. If you're lucky enough to have a coffee roaster nearby, you're going to get freshly roasted beans; otherwise you might want to consider mail order.

Some people like the automatic drip coffee makers. Others, claiming to be coffee purists, prefer to pour the hot water over the grounds into a carafe. Either way, make sure you have the right kind of filter. (We know you can use a paper towel in a pinch, but don't make a habit of it.)

Grinding just enough beans for your current needs means you'll have fresher tasting coffee. Small coffee bean grinders are affordable and easy to find. Keep the beans in an airtight container, away from light and moisture, until you need them. Adding a little cinnamon to the grounds will take out some of the bitterness.

A few coffee houses to try: Bongo Java, Nashville, Tennessee; Kramerbooks and Afterwords, Washington, DC; Brazil, Houston, Texas; and Caffé Dante, New York. Scour your own city for a coffee house hangout, à la Central Perk. You never know who might drop by.

Phoebe:
If you want, call her machine. If she has a lot of beeps, it probably means she hasn't picked up her messages yet.

Chandler:
You don't think that seems a little—

Ross:
Desperate? Needy? Pathetic?

Chandler:
You obviously saw my personal ad.

Classic Cappuccino

This Italian coffee drink is easy to prepare if you have the right equipment. An espresso/cappuccino machine that has a steaming wand for frothing milk is your best bet. A cheaper option is a stovetop espresso maker (one of those shiny metal Italian coffee pots that sits right on the burner) and a separate milk steamer. Rinse the cup or mug you are using with hot tap water to keep the espresso warm while you froth the milk. Either way, follow this recipe and you'll impress your friends—and yourself—to no end.

1½ **ounces brewed espresso**
   Sugar
3 **ounces cold milk**
   Ground cinnamon or cocoa, optional

▶ Prepare a single espresso and pour it into a warmed 6-ounce cup or mug. Stir in sugar to taste. Pour the milk into a small metal pitcher and froth until dense. Do not steam the milk so much that it becomes stiff or dry. Properly steamed milk is thick but still soft. Pour the steamed milk into the cup with the espresso, filling it almost to the rim. Use a spoon to float some frothed milk on top. Sprinkle the milk foam with cinnamon or cocoa, if desired, and drink up immediately. (To make 2 cappuccinos, prepare a double espresso and steam twice as much milk. With most espresso machines, you will have to grind more coffee and start again to make more than 2 espresso drinks.)

Serves 1

Spiced Hot Cider

When the wind is howling and the snow is blowing, hot cider is a great way to warm up. Spike mugs of spiced cider with rum just before serving, if you like.

4 **cups apple cider**
2 **cinnamon sticks**
4 **whole cloves**
2 **cardamom pods**
1 **orange**

▶ Place the cider and spices in a medium saucepan. Use a vegetable peeler to remove the colored skin from the orange, leaving behind the bitter white pith. Add the pieces of peel to the pot. (Remove the stringy, white pith with your hand and eat the orange, if you like.)

▶ Bring the cider to a boil and simmer gently for 5 minutes. Use a slotted spoon to fish out the spices and the orange peel. (The cinnamon sticks can be saved and used as a garnish/stirrer for the cups of cider; the other spices and orange peel should be thrown out.) Pour the cider into mugs and enjoy before a roaring fire.

Serves 6

"Ugly Naked Guy has a hula hoop!**"**

Espresso Granita

Granita is a type of Italian ice that can be made in the freezer by scraping the ice crystals with a spoon as they set. Serve this version (nothing more than frozen espresso) on a long hot summer's night when you're up late gazing at the stars or spying on the Ugly Naked Guy. It's impossible to fall asleep after enjoying something this cold and caffeinated. Two cups of strong brewed coffee may be used in place of the espresso and water, if desired. Of course, decaffeinated espresso/coffee should be used if you plan on snoozing anytime soon.

I	**cup brewed espresso**
¼	**cup sugar**
I	**cup cold water**

► Pour the hot espresso into a bowl and add the sugar. Stir briskly until the sugar has dissolved. Stir in the cold water. Cool to room temperature.

► Pour the mixture into a 2-inch-deep pan that measures about 13 inches long and 9 inches across. Place the pan in the freezer for 30 minutes. Stir the frozen crystals from around the edges of the pan back into the liquid. As the mixture continues to freeze, scrape a spoon against the sides and bottom of the pan to loosen and break up any frozen crystals. Repeat the scraping process every 30 minutes or so until the mixture is frozen and a bit creamy, about 3 hours total. Scoop the frozen crystals into individual bowls or goblets and serve immediately.

Serves 4

Lemon-Ginger Iced Tea

There's more to life than coffee. There's tea, for instance. This iced tea is a refreshing, caffeine-free way to quench your thirst.

4	**cups water**
2	**large lemons**
I	**2-inch knob fresh ginger root**
¼	**cup sugar, or more to taste**
	Ice cubes

► Bring the water to a boil in a medium saucepan. While you are waiting for the water to boil, halve 1 of the lemons and squeeze its juice into the pan. (It's okay if the pits end up in the water, too.) Add the squeezed lemon halves to the pan.

► The next step is to grate the ginger. There's no need to peel the ginger; just grate it on the fine holes of a box grater. There should be about 3 tablespoons grated ginger. Add the ginger to the water and simmer for 15 minutes. Strain the tea through a mesh strainer or a colander lined with paper towels. Stir in the sugar until dissolved.

► Refrigerate the tea until well chilled. Thinly slice the second lemon. Serve the tea over ice in tall glasses garnished with lemon slices.

Serves 6

Rachel:
Okay, I checked. We have: Earl Grey, English Breakfast, Chamomile, Cinnamon Stick, Mint Medley, Blackberry, and wait, there's one more . . . Lemon Soother. You're not the guy who asked for the tea, are you?

Monica:
We thought since Phoebe was staying over, we'd make it kind of a slumber party thing. We got trashy magazines, we got cookie dough, we got Twister—

Phoebe:
Oooh! And I brought Operation—but I lost the tweezers, so we can't operate. But we can prep the guy.

Hot Chocolate, Italian Style

Coffee houses in Italy serve this hot, creamy drink made with chocolate bars (not cocoa powder) throughout the winter. Trendy American coffee houses have followed suit. Order a *cioccolata calda con panna* (hot chocolate with cream) the next time you're coffee house hopping, if you really want to impress your friends.

1⅓ cups milk
2 tablespoons sugar
1½ teaspoons cornstarch
4 ounces best-quality bittersweet or semisweet chocolate, chopped
Whipped cream (at least 1 tablespoon per serving or more)

▶ Place the milk in a small saucepan. Whisk in the sugar and cornstarch; then add the chopped chocolate. Turn the heat to medium and stir constantly until the chocolate melts and the mixture comes to a boil. Simmer for 30 seconds, stirring constantly, and then remove the pan from the heat. Pour the hot chocolate into cups (large coffee cups or the bowl-shaped cups used for latte are perfect). Dollop each cup with some whipped cream and serve immediately.

Serves 2

Chewy Molasses Cookies

Soft and chewy, these spice cookies are best with a latte on a cold winter day. A touch of molasses gives these large cookies their rich flavor.

1 cup flour
¾ teaspoon ground ginger
½ teaspoon ground cinnamon
¼ teaspoon salt
¼ teaspoon baking soda
6 tablespoons unsalted butter, melted
½ cup sugar
2 tablespoons molasses
1 large egg

▶ Preheat the oven to 350°. Stir the flour, spices, salt, and baking soda together in a small bowl.

▶ Mix the melted butter with the sugar and molasses in a large bowl. Lightly beat the egg with a fork and stir it into the butter-sugar mixture. Gently stir in the dry ingredients. The batter will be fairly wet.

▶ Line 2 large baking sheets with aluminum foil. Drop the batter by rounded tablespoons onto the foil, leaving at least 2 inches between each ball of dough.

▶ Bake until the cookies firm up and the edges begin to darken slightly, 10 to 12 minutes. Remove the baking sheets from the oven and transfer the cookies on the foil to racks. Cool for several minutes; then carefully peel the cookies off the foil.

Makes 18 large, flat cookies

Italian Almond Biscotti

Roger:
Listen, guys, it was great seeing you again. And Mon, easy on those cookies, okay? Remember, they're just food. They're not love.

Biscotti, which means "twice cooked" in Italian, must bake longer than most cookies. However, there is no need to divide dough into individual portions or stand by the oven and make batch after batch. Just shape the dough into long logs and then slice into individual cookies after the first baking. The biscotti are then baked again for 5 minutes to crisp the edges. This version has no butter and is particularly crunchy. A quick dunk in some coffee will soften them right up.

¾   **cup whole almonds with skin**

1½   **cups flour**

½   **teaspoon baking powder**

⅛   **teaspoon salt**

1   **cup sugar**

3   **large eggs**

1   **teaspoon vanilla extract**

▶ Preheat the oven to 350°. Spread the almonds out on a large baking sheet and toast them in the oven for 5 minutes. Cool the almonds and then chop them roughly.

▶ Stir the flour, baking powder, salt, and sugar together in a large bowl. Use your hands to make a well in the dry ingredients. (This is like digging out a hole in the sand at the beach.) Crack 2 eggs into the well. Add the vanilla and use a fork (and then your hands) to mix well. If the dough seems wet, knead in some more flour. When the dough is smooth (it should also be fairly stiff and dry), work in the nuts with your hands.

▶ Grease and then flour a large baking sheet. Turn the dough out onto a floured counter. Divide the dough in half and roll each half into a log that measures about 12 inches long and 2 inches wide. Transfer the logs to the prepared baking sheet, leaving at least 2 inches between the logs.

▶ Beat the remaining egg with a fork. Brush the beaten egg over the logs. (This will give them a shiny coating when baked.) Bake the logs until golden brown, 30 to 35 minutes. Remove the baking sheet from the oven. Wearing an oven mitt or other protective gear to hold the logs in place, use a serrated knife to cut them crosswise on the diagonal into ¾-inch-thick cookies.

▶ Lay the cookies on one side and return the baking sheet to the oven. Toast until the biscotti are crisp, 5 to 10 minutes. Cool the biscotti on racks and store in an airtight container for weeks.

Makes 18 long biscotti

"L*et's just say my Curious George doll is no longer curious.***"**

Cappuccino Biscotti with Chocolate Chips

In this version, the biscotti are flavored with milk and espresso and then loaded with plenty of chocolate chips.

2	**cups flour**
1	**cup sugar**
½	**teaspoon ground cinnamon**
½	**teaspoon baking powder**
½	**teaspoon baking soda**
½	**teaspoon salt**
2	**tablespoons milk**
¼	**cup brewed espresso or strong coffee, cooled slightly**
1	**large egg yolk**
1	**teaspoon vanilla extract**
⅔	**cup whole almonds, chopped coarse**
½	**cup semisweet chocolate chips**

▶ Preheat the oven to 375°. Blend the flour, sugar, cinnamon, baking powder, baking soda, and salt briefly with an electric mixer.

▶ Stir the milk into the espresso along with the egg yolk and vanilla. Mix well and then add to the dry ingredients. Beat until the dough is smooth, about 1 minute. Stir in the nuts and chocolate chips.

▶ Grease and then flour a large baking sheet. Turn the dough out onto a floured counter. Divide the dough in half and roll each half into a log that measures about 12 inches long and 2 inches wide. Transfer the logs to the prepared baking sheet, leaving at least 2 inches between the logs.

▶ Bake until the logs are firm to the touch, about 30 minutes. Remove the baking sheet from the oven and reduce the temperature to 325°. Wearing an oven mitt to hold the logs in place, use a serrated knife to cut them crosswise on the diagonal into ¾-inch-thick cookies.

▶ Lay the cookies on one side and return the baking sheet to the oven. Bake until the biscotti are crisp, 5 to 10 minutes. Cool the biscotti on racks and store in an airtight container.

Makes 24 long biscotti

BISCOTTI
Crisp cookies often containing almonds or filberts. Italian, from Medieval Latin *bis coctus*, or twice cooked.

Rachel on Work

"Look look look look look! My first paycheck. Look at the little window. There's my name. Hi, me! Isn't this exciting! I earned this. I wiped tables for it, I steamed milk for it, and it's—not worth it. Who's FICA? Why is he getting my money?"

"Go, Monana! Well, you ladies are not the only ones living the dream. I get to go pour coffee for people I don't know. Don't wait up."

"Excuse me, sir. You come in here all the time. I was just wondering . . . do you think there's a possibility of you giving me an advance on my tips?"

"Oh. Wish me luck. I'm going to get one of those job things."

Jennifer Aniston / RACHEL

Jennifer Aniston has appeared in several television series, including *The Edge, Sunday Funnies, Ferris Bueller,* and *Molloy*. Additionally, she starred in *Camp Cucamonga* and guest starred on such series as *Burke's Law, Quantum Leap,* and *Herman's Head*. Among her stage credits are *For Dear Life* at the New York Shakespeare Festival and *Dancing on Checker's Grave*. Raised in the Big Apple, Aniston made her feature film debut in *Leprechaun*. She is no stranger to acting, because her father, John Aniston, stars in *Days of Our Lives*.

Pine Nut Cookies

Chewy almond cookies covered with pine nuts are a classic in Italy and in trendy coffee bars from Seattle to New York. Homemade almond paste—nothing more than blanched almonds, sugar, and egg whites—is the basis for these pine-nut covered clusters. For a dressier look, sift confectioners' sugar over the cookies after they come out of the oven.

1 ⅔	**cups blanched slivered almonds**
1 ⅓	**cups sugar**
2	**large egg whites**
1	**cup pine nuts**

► Preheat the oven to 375°. Grease 2 large baking sheets and set them aside.

► Place the almonds and sugar in the work bowl of a food processor and grind until quite fine. Add the egg whites and process until the mixture is smooth. (The dough will be wet and sticky.) Scrape the dough into a bowl. Pour the pine nuts into a shallow bowl.

► Take a rounded tablespoon of the batter and shape it into a rough ball about the size of a whole walnut. (Working with this batter will take you back to your Play-Doh days.) Roll each ball in the pine nuts just until the outside is covered. Place the pine-nut covered balls on prepared baking sheets, leaving 2 inches between each ball.

► Bake until the cookies turn light golden brown in color, 13 to 15 minutes. Do not let nuts burn or turn dark brown. Cool the cookies on a rack.

Makes 18 large cookies

Pecan Coffee Cake

This quick cake is perfect for satisfying a morning craving. It's also a great accompaniment for an afternoon coffee or tea break. If you like, walnuts may be used in place of pecans.

Pecan Topping

½   **cup firmly packed light brown sugar**
½   **cup finely chopped pecans**
2   **tablespoons flour**
I   **teaspoon ground cinnamon**
2   **tablespoons unsalted butter, softened**

Coffee Cake

8   **tablespoons (I stick) unsalted butter, softened**
I   **cup firmly packed light brown sugar**
2   **large eggs**
I½   **cups flour**
I½   **teaspoons baking powder**
½   **teaspoon salt**
½   **cup milk**

▶ Preheat the oven to 375°. Grease a 9-inch-square cake pan and set it aside.

▶ Mix the topping ingredients with your fingers or a fork until the butter is cut into very small pieces and coated with sugar and nuts. Set the mixture aside.

▶ Cream the butter and sugar with an electric mixer until light and fluffy, about 1 minute. Add the eggs and beat until the batter is smooth, 1 to 2 minutes.

▶ Stir the flour, baking powder, and salt together in a small bowl. Add the dry ingredients to the batter alternately with some of the milk. Mix until the batter is smooth. Pour the batter into the prepared pan and sprinkle evenly with the reserved topping.

▶ Bake until a toothpick inserted in the center of the cake comes out clean and the edges begin to pull away from the sides of the pan, about 30 minutes. Cool pan briefly on a rack. Cut the cake into squares and serve warm.

Serves 8

Nana's Cinnamon-Scented Coffee

Ross and Monica's grandmother had a real passion for Sweet 'N Low. She stole pink packets from restaurants and relatives' homes and stored them in boxes, the bottom of her purse—everywhere. A little ground cinnamon gives this regular brewed coffee an old-fashioned flavor. Nana sweetened coffee with "the pink stuff," but you can use sugar if you prefer.

I   **cup ground coffee**
½   **teaspoon ground cinnamon**
6   **cups cold water**
    Milk or half-and-half as desired
    Sweet 'N Low or sugar as desired

▶ Place the ground coffee in a filter. Sprinkle the cinnamon over the grounds. Brew coffee with the amount of water indicated above. Serve hot coffee with milk and sweetener.

Fills 6 good-sized cups or mugs

Rachel:
I was laughed out of twelve interviews today.

Chandler:
And yet you're surprisingly upbeat.

Rachel:
Well, you would be, too, if you found Joan and David boots on sale fifty percent off.

Joey:
It's never gonna happen.

Ross:
What?

Joey:
You and Rachel.

Ross:
*Wha— Me and Ra—?
You think I— Wha—?
Why not?*

Joey:
*Because, you waited too
long to make your move,
and now you're in the
"Friend Zone."*

Ross:
*No, no, no. I'm not in the
Zone.*

Joey:
*Ross, you're mayor of the
Zone.*

Trendy Tiramisù

This classic Italian dessert is popular
in restaurants across the nation,
including those in New York's Little
Italy. There's no baking involved.
Simply layer espresso-soaked Italian
cookies with a rich mascarpone (an
Italian cream cheese) filling and dust
with bittersweet chocolate. The
name of this dessert translates as
"pick me up" and no doubt refers to
the coffee jolt.

6   **large eggs, separated**

3   **tablespoons sugar**

I   **pound mascarpone cheese (available at
    Italian and gourmet stores)**

2   **tablespoons brandy or coffee-flavored
    liqueur**

I   **teaspoon vanilla extract**

1½ **cups brewed espresso or very strong coffee,
    cooled**

30 **Italian ladyfingers (these long, crisp
    cookies are also sold at Italian and
    gourmet stores)**

8   **ounces bittersweet chocolate, chopped fine**

▶ Beat the egg yolks and sugar
  with an electric mixer until light
  yellow in color, about 1 minute.
  Beat in the mascarpone, brandy,
  and vanilla extract until smooth.
  Beat the egg whites in a separate
  bowl with an electric mixer until
  stiff but not dry. Gently fold the
  whites into the mascarpone
  mixture and set aside briefly.

▶ Pour the cooled espresso into a
  wide, shallow bowl. Dip the
  ladyfingers into the espresso 1 at
  a time and arrange them in a
  13x9-inch pan. Use half of the
  cookies to cover the bottom of
  the pan.

▶ Spread half of the mascarpone
  mixture over the cookies and
  then sprinkle with half of the
  chocolate. Dip the remaining
  cookies in the espresso and make
  a second layer of cookies on top
  of the chocolate. Spread the
  remaining mascarpone mixture
  over the second layer of cookies
  and then sprinkle with the
  remaining chocolate.

▶ Cover the pan tightly with plastic
  wrap and refrigerate for at least 4
  hours to allow cookies to soften.
  Tiramisù may be refrigerated for
  up to 8 hours.

Serves 8 to 10

MASCARPONE
**A fresh, soft Italian cheese with a high
butterfat content, made from cow's milk
enriched with cream.**

Comfort Foods

Eating for physical and emotional sustenance

Monica:
This is so typical. We give and we give and we give and then we just get nothing back. And then, one day, you just wake up and say, "See you around." Let's go, Phoebe.

Phoebe:
You know what, we thought you were different. But I guess it was just the coma.

Grown-Up Grilled Cheese

Even Monica herself couldn't make a better grilled cheese. Dress up this childhood classic by using mozzarella cheese and basil. Eat it when you're lonely.

¼   **pound mozzarella cheese (Monica would never use anything but fresh mozzarella packed in water), sliced thin**

I   **large tomato, sliced thin**

4   **large slices of sourdough or crusty peasant bread**

      Salt and ground black pepper

      Small handful whole fresh basil leaves

¼   **cup olive oil**

▶ Layer the cheese and tomato over 2 slices of bread. Sprinkle with salt and pepper to taste and top each with several basil leaves. Cover with the remaining slices of bread to form sandwiches.

▶ Heat 2 tablespoons oil in a large skillet set over medium heat. Add the sandwiches and cook, pressing down on them with a spatula, until the bottoms are golden brown. Flip the sandwiches, and add the remaining 2 tablespoons oil.

▶ Continue cooking, occasionally pressing down on sandwiches with a spatula, until the other slices of bread are golden brown and the cheese has melted. Remove the sandwiches from the pan, cut them in half, and eat immediately.

Serves 2

Rich and Creamy Chocolate Pudding

What is it that's so comforting about eating foods with a spoon? It probably has something to do with happy childhood memories, when life's biggest dilemma was chocolate or vanilla. This rich, dark chocolate pudding will satisfy kids and adults who know that chocolate is the answer to any problem.

½   **cup sugar**

⅓   **cup unsweetened cocoa**

2   **tablespoons cornstarch**

2   **cups milk**

2   **ounces semisweet or bittersweet chocolate**

2   **tablespoons unsalted butter**

I   **teaspoon vanilla extract**

▶ Whisk the sugar, cocoa, and cornstarch together in a medium saucepan to break up any lumps. Slowly whisk in the milk and set the pan over medium heat. Bring the mixture to a boil, stirring often, especially as the mixture thickens and becomes very hot. Simmer gently for 1 minute, stirring constantly to prevent scorching.

▶ Stir in the semisweet chocolate and butter. When they have melted, remove the pan from the heat and stir in the vanilla. Pour the pudding into 4 custard cups or small bowls. Cool slightly and serve warm (if you like soft pudding), or chill in the refrigerator (if you prefer it cold and creamy).

Serves 4

Rachel's Soothing Chicken Soup

Nervous about your upcoming nuptials? Abandoned at the altar? This chicken soup will calm frayed nerves, whatever the cause.

3	**pounds chicken wings, backs, and thighs (any combination will do)**
1	**large onion, peeled**
2	**ribs celery with leaves, cut in half**
6	**medium carrots, peeled and cut into 2-inch lengths**
2	**medium parsnips, peeled**
1	**small bunch fresh dill**
1	**medium bunch fresh Italian parsley**
3	**quarts cold water**
	Salt and ground white pepper
12	**medium matzoh balls or 3 cups cooked small pasta shape, such as stars, orzo, or tiny elbows**

▶ Rinse the chicken parts under cold, running water. Place the damp chicken in a large stock pot or soup kettle along with the onion, celery, carrots, parsnips, dill, and parsley. Add the water. Bring to a boil and simmer, occasionally skimming foam from surface, for 1 hour.

▶ While the soup is cooking, prepare the matzoh balls according to package directions, or boil and drain a small pasta shape. Strain the soup, and discard the solids except for the carrots. Return the carrots to the pot and set it over low heat. Add salt and white pepper to taste. Add the matzoh balls or cooked pasta and bring to a gentle simmer. Ladle the hot soup in large bowls. Extra portions can be refrigerated for several days.

Serves 6

Mashed Potatoes for the Broken Hearted

These fluffy, smooth potatoes (with plenty of sour cream and butter) have been known to mend even the most fractured heart. Your doctor may disagree, but this is what Mom surely would prescribe (if only you'd call her more often).

2	**pounds russet or baking potatoes, peeled and cut into 2-inch pieces**
	Salt
4	**tablespoons butter**
¾	**cup sour cream**
	Ground black pepper

▶ Place the potatoes into a large saucepan and cover with cold water. Add salt to taste and bring to a boil. Simmer for 20 minutes or until the potatoes are tender. Drain the potatoes and return them to the saucepan set over low heat. Work the potatoes with a masher until smooth. Stir in the butter and sour cream. Keep the pan over the burner until the butter has melted. Season with salt and pepper and serve immediately.

Serves 4

M A T Z O H
A brittle, flat piece of unleavened bread, eaten especially during Passover.

Ross:
So, uh, Rachel. What are you, uh, doing tonight?

Rachel:
Big glamour night. Me and Monica at Launderama.

Monica:
Is it me? Is it like I have a beacon that only dogs and men with severe emotional problems can hear?

Misery Meatloaf

When romance hits the rocks, the unlucky-in-love invariably turn to food. Chocolate often helps, but you can't eat it for dinner every night. This all-American meatloaf, accompanied by creamy mashed potatoes, will make even the worst break-up seem manageable.

2	**pounds ground meat (use all beef or get a mixture of beef, veal, and pork, often called "meatloaf mixture" by butchers)**
1	**medium onion, minced**
1	**tablespoon Worcestershire sauce**
½	**cup ketchup**
1	**teaspoon salt**
½	**teaspoon ground black pepper**
2	**eggs**
2	**slices white bread, crusts removed**
½	**cup milk**
2	**teaspoons spicy brown mustard**
2	**tablespoons brown sugar**

▶ Preheat the oven to 375°. Mix the ground meat, onion, Worcestershire sauce, ¼ cup ketchup, salt, pepper, and eggs in a large bowl. Soak the bread in a small bowl with the milk for several minutes. Crumble the slices of bread and work them into the meat mixture.

▶ Shape the mixture into a rough loaf shape and place it on a large baking sheet. Bake for 45 minutes.

▶ While the meatloaf is in the oven, stir together the remaining ¼ cup ketchup, mustard, and brown sugar. Brush the glaze over the meatloaf and continue cooking until the juices run clear when the meatloaf is skewered, about 15 minutes more. Slice and serve with mashed potatoes.

Serves 4 to 6

Mrs. Trib's Roast Chicken

Joey's mom (as played by Brenda Vaccaro) still brings groceries when she comes to visit, even if she does smack Joey in the head with her big ol' ring. Here, the fixings that might be found in her sacks.

1	**roasting chicken (about 5 pounds), rinsed and patted dry**
4	**medium cloves garlic, sliced thin**
4	**sprigs fresh rosemary**
1	**large lemon**
	Salt and ground black pepper

▶ Preheat the oven to 400°. Place the chicken in a large roasting pan. Lift the skin from around the breast and thigh (without tearing it) and slip garlic slices between the meat and skin. Slide 1 rosemary sprig under the skin on each breast and place the remaining 2 sprigs in the bird's cavity. Halve the lemon and squeeze the juices over the chicken. Place the lemon halves in the cavity. Season the skin and cavity well with salt and pepper to taste.

▶ Roast the chicken, basting occasionally, until the leg juices run clear when pierced with a knife, about 1½ hours. Carve the chicken and serve with potatoes or rice.

Serves 4 to 6

Comfort Foods

Adults Only Macaroni and Cheese

Macaroni and cheese from a box might be fine for kids, but adult troubles need a homemade touch. A piping hot plate of these noodles and cheese will cheer up even your most depressed friend.

1	**cup milk**
3	**tablespoons butter**
1½	**tablespoons flour**
½	**pound sharp Cheddar cheese, shredded**
	Salt
	Dash of cayenne pepper
½	**pound macaroni elbows**
¼	**cup plain bread crumbs**

▶ Preheat the oven to 375°. Lightly grease a 2-quart casserole dish and set it aside.

▶ Heat the milk in a small pan until warm. Meanwhile, melt 2 tablespoons butter in a small skillet until foamy. Stir in the flour and cook for 2 minutes. Slowly whisk in the milk until smooth. Continue cooking over low heat until the sauce thickens to the consistency of cream, about 5 minutes. Add the cheese, salt to taste, and cayenne pepper. Stir until the cheese melts. Cover and keep the sauce warm.

▶ Cook and drain the macaroni. Mix the macaroni and hot cheese sauce in the prepared casserole dish. Sprinkle the bread crumbs over the top and dot with the remaining tablespoon of butter that has been cut into very small pieces.

▶ Bake until the cheese is bubbling and the top is golden brown, 25 to 30 minutes. Spoon out onto large plates.

Serves 2

Blueberry-Cinnamon Sundae

This seemingly rich sundae is just the ticket when you want something sweet without loads of fat. Save any extra sauce and frozen yogurt for another day. Tomorrow, maybe?

1	**cup blueberries**
1	**tablespoon sugar or more to taste**
1	**tablespoon water**
¼	**teaspoon ground cinnamon**
1	**pint vanilla frozen yogurt**

▶ Toss the berries with the sugar, water, and cinnamon in a small saucepan. Set the pan over medium heat and bring the liquid to a boil. Lightly mash some of the berries with a fork and continue simmering until the juices thicken a bit, about 1 minute. Remove the pan from the heat and let the sauce cool for a couple of minutes.

▶ Scoop the frozen yogurt into 2 bowls. Spoon the warm blueberry sauce over each portion and serve immediately.

Makes 2 large sundaes

Ross:
Oh, Pheebs, I'm sorry. I've gotta go. I've got Lamaze class.

Chandler:
Oh, and I've got Earth Science. But, I'll catch you in Gym?

Joey:
You know there already is a Joseph Stalin?

Chandler:
You're kidding.

Joey:
Apparently, he was this Russian dictator who slaughtered all these people. You'd think you would've known that.

Chandler:
You know, you'd think I would've.

Rice Pudding with Raisins

Rice pudding is the quintessential New York comfort food. It seems as though every deli in town makes some version of this homey dessert. On a snowy winter's night when it's simply too cold to venture outdoors, try making your own. And remember: A dollop of whipped cream never hurts.

3½   **cups milk**
⅓   **cup long-grain rice**
⅓   **cup raisins**
¼   **cup sugar**
1   **teaspoon vanilla extract**
    Dash of ground cinnamon (an authentic but optional touch)
    Whipped cream, optional

▶   Stir the milk, rice, raisins, and sugar together in a medium saucepan. Bring the mixture to a boil, stirring occasionally. Reduce the heat to medium and partially cover.

▶   Gently simmer the pudding, stirring often, until most of the milk has been absorbed, 25 to 30 minutes. Remove the pan from the heat and stir in the vanilla.

▶   Pour the rice pudding into 4 custard cups or small bowls. Sprinkle each with cinnamon, if desired. Cool slightly and serve warm or chilled with whipped cream if you like.

Serves 4

Decadent Sundae

This sundae combines three of the world's best feel-good flavors—chocolate, vanilla, and peanut butter—in one outrageous dessert. If you are wallowing alone in your misery, store any extra sauce in the refrigerator until the next crisis, which could be as soon as your next job interview.

3   **tablespoons unsweetened cocoa**
¼   **cup sugar**
¼   **cup heavy cream**
1   **tablespoon smooth peanut butter**
1   **pint vanilla ice cream or other favorite flavor**
    Whipped cream and chopped nuts (optional, unless you are really depressed, in which case they are essential)

▶   Stir the cocoa and sugar together in a small saucepan to remove any lumps. Slowly whisk in the cream until smooth. Set the pan over medium heat. Bring the sauce to the barest simmer, stirring occasionally to dissolve the sugar. At the first sign of a boil, remove the pan from the heat and stir in the peanut butter until smooth.

▶   Scoop the ice cream into 2 bowls and drizzle each portion with several tablespoons of the sauce. Add whipped cream and chopped nuts, if desired. Serve immediately.

Makes 2 large sundaes

Savory Corn Muffins

These savory muffins can be served as a soothing start to the day or as an accompaniment to chili. If you like, add jalapeño peppers to spice things up a bit.

1	**cup flour**
¾	**cup cornmeal**
1	**tablespoon baking powder**
½	**teaspoon salt**
10	**tablespoons (1¼ sticks) unsalted butter, melted**
1	**large egg**
1¼	**cups milk, warmed slightly**
1 or 2	**jalapeño peppers, stemmed and minced (optional)**

▶ Preheat the oven to 375°. Grease a regular 12-cup muffin tin and set it aside.

▶ Stir together the flour, cornmeal, baking powder, and salt in a medium bowl and set it aside. Beat the melted butter and egg in a large bowl until well combined. Stir in the warm milk. Fold in the dry ingredients (as well as the peppers, if using) until just blended. Do not overmix.

▶ Spoon the batter into the prepared muffin tin, filling the cups almost to the brim. Bake until the muffins are golden brown and a toothpick inserted in the center comes out clean, 20 to 25 minutes. Cool the muffins in the tin for 5 minutes, turn them out onto a rack, and eat them as soon as you can.

Makes 12 muffins

Chandler's Cinnamon Toast

Chandler is the first to admit that his culinary repertoire is quite limited. But apparently he is familiar with toast, and we bet even he could pull off this fancy version.

4	**tablespoons (½ stick) unsalted butter, melted**
3	**tablespoons sugar**
1	**teaspoon ground cinnamon**
8	**slices white bread**

▶ Preheat the broiler. Stir the melted butter, sugar, and cinnamon together in a small bowl. Place the bread on a large baking sheet and toast both sides under the broiler. Brush the melted butter mixture over the top of the bread slices and eat immediately.

Serves 4

Monica:
Would you let it go? It's not that big a deal.

Ross:
Not that big a deal? It's amazing! You just reach in, there's one little maneuver, and BAM! A bra! Right out the sleeve! As far as I'm concerned, there is nothing a guy can do that even comes close.

Rachel:
Oh, come on! You guys can pee standing up.

Chandler:
We can? Okay, I'm trying that.

Monica:
*There's nothing to tell.
He's just some guy I work
with.*

Joey:
*Come on. You're goin'
out with the guy. There's
gotta be somethin'
wrong with him.*

Chandler:
*So, does he have a
hump? A hump and a
hairpiece?*

Phoebe:
*Wait. Does he eat chalk?
Just 'cause I don't want
her to go through what I
went through with Carl.*

Monica:
*Okay everybody. Relax.
This is not even a date.
It's just two people going
out to dinner and not
having sex.*

Chandler:
Sounds like a date to me.

Call-Back Spaghetti and Meatballs

While Joey waits for his big break, he can take comfort in a heaping plate of spaghetti and meatballs. Lots of grated cheese, and the promise of another audition, keep even the most anxious actor going strong.

1	**pound ground beef**
⅔	**cup grated Parmesan cheese, plus plenty for the table**
½	**cup plain bread crumbs**
1	**teaspoon dried oregano**
1½	**teaspoons salt**
½	**teaspoon ground black pepper**
2	**large eggs**
	Oil for cooking the meatballs
3	**cups favorite tomato sauce**
1	**pound spaghetti**

▶ Mix the beef, ⅔ cup cheese, bread crumbs, oregano, salt, pepper, and eggs in a large bowl. When the ingredients are well combined, break off large clumps to form 1-inch meatballs.

▶ Heat ½ inch oil in a large skillet set over medium-high heat. Add as many meatballs as can fit in 1 layer. Cook, turning occasionally, until the meatballs are nicely browned and cooked through, 8 to 10 minutes. Use a slotted spoon to transfer the browned meatballs to a plate lined with paper towels. Repeat the process with the remaining meatballs.

▶ Heat the tomato sauce in a medium saucepan. Add the meatballs and simmer gently while you cook and drain the spaghetti. Toss the pasta with a little of the tomato sauce, and divide it among individual plates. Ladle the remaining sauce and meatballs over the spaghetti. Serve with lots of grated cheese, and just a touch of sympathy.

Serves 4

Stay at Home Pasta

This sauce has so much garlic it has been reported to break up even rock-solid relationships. But when it's just the guys or girls gathered around the table for a bite, nothing is more satisfying than a bowl of pasta.

1	**pound spaghetti or linguine**
⅓	**cup olive oil**
10	**medium cloves garlic, minced**
3	**tablespoons minced fresh parsley leaves**
1	**teaspoon salt or to taste**
	Ground black pepper

▶ First things first. Bring water to a boil for cooking the pasta. Add the pasta and stir whenever.

▶ While the pasta is cooking, heat the oil in a skillet. Add the garlic and sauté over medium-low heat until richly colored but not burned, about 5 minutes. The garlic must be golden (or it will be raw-tasting) but should not be brown (it will become bitter).

▶ Stir the parsley, salt, and pepper to taste into the garlic sauce. Cook for another 30 seconds or so. Take the pan off the heat and wait for the pasta to finish cooking. When the pasta is how you like it, drain and toss it with the garlic sauce.

Serves 4

Chandler on Dating

"She's amazing. She makes the women I dream about look like short, fat, bald men."

"Sometimes I wish I was a lesbian. Did I say that out loud?"

"Excuse me. You don't think I could get a Brian? Because I could get a Brian. Believe you me."

"All right, somebody kiss me. Somebody kiss me. It's midnight. Kiss me. Somebody kiss me."

"I hit her in the eye! I hit her in the eye! This is the worst breakup in the history of the world!"

"I'm not going to talk to her. She obviously got the message. And is choosing not to call me. Now I'm needy and snubbed. God, I miss just being needy."

"Hi. Um, I'm account number 714357457. And, uh, I don't know if you got any of that, but I would really like a copy of the tape."

Cornmeal-Buttermilk Waffles

These waffles are delicious and have very little fat. If you don't own a waffle iron, ask your mother to check the attic. Homemade waffles really are much better (and more grown-up) than waffles that pop out of a toaster.

¾ **cup flour**
¼ **cup cornmeal**
1 **teaspoon baking soda**
½ **teaspoon salt**
1 **cup buttermilk**
1 **tablespoon vegetable oil**
2 **large egg whites**
    Nonstick vegetable oil spray

▶ Okay, so you really do have a waffle iron. Plug it in and let it heat up while you make the batter.

▶ Stir together the dry ingredients in a large bowl. Mix the buttermilk and oil in a measuring cup with a fork. Beat the egg whites with an electric mixer until they form stiff peaks, about 1 minute. (You can beat the egg whites by hand with a whisk; it's good exercise for your forearm, especially if you've avoided the gym this week.)

▶ Slowly stir the buttermilk mixture into the dry ingredients and blend with a spatula until smooth. Gently fold in the stiff egg whites. Do not overmix; less stirring is definitely better.

▶ Lightly grease the waffle iron grids with vegetable oil spray. Pour about ½ cup batter into the preheated waffle iron. The batter is fairly thick, so you might need to spread it with a spoon to cover the grid evenly. Close the waffle iron and cook until the waffle is crisp, 3 to 4 minutes.

▶ Remove the waffle and serve with jam, honey, syrup, or fruit. Make more waffles as you eat. (This is really a two-person operation; one person eats, while the other cooks. Be sure to switch off occasionally; it's only fair.)

Makes 4 waffles, enough for 2

*"*R*oss, he's playing with my spatulas again."*

Matthew Perry / CHANDLER

Matthew Perry, who grew up in Ottawa, has starred as a series regular in several comedies, including *Homefree*, *Sydney*, and *Boys Will Be Boys* and in a recurring role on *Growing Pains*. He also starred in *Deadly Relations*, *Call Me Anna*, and *Dance Til Dawn* and guest starred on *Beverly Hills, 90210*, *Who's the Boss?*, *Empty Nest*, *Just the Ten of Us*, *Highway to Heaven*, *Charles in Charge*, *The Tracey Ullman Show*, and *Silver Spoons*. Among Perry's motion picture credits are *A Night in the Life of Jimmy Reardon*, *She's Out of Control*, and *Parallel Lives*. Perry is the son of John Bennett Perry, known for his Old Spice commercials.

Aurora's Pancakes

When it comes time for Chandler to fix breakfast for an overnight guest, he runs across the hall. Luckily, Monica has some pancake mix. Maybe if Chandler had made these pancakes from scratch, Aurora would have stayed over again.

1½	**cups flour**
1	**teaspoon salt**
2	**tablespoons sugar**
2	**teaspoons baking powder**
1¼	**cups milk**
2	**large eggs**
4	**tablespoons (½ stick) butter, melted, plus extra for the pan**

▶ Combine the flour, salt, sugar, and baking powder in a large bowl, using a whisk to remove any lumps.

▶ Pour the milk into a large glass measuring cup. Add the eggs and butter and beat with a fork until smooth. Slowly stir the wet ingredients into the dry ingredients using a rubber spatula. Do not overmix the batter.

▶ Heat a griddle or large skillet. Grease the pan with a little butter. Drop several tablespoons of batter onto the pan for each pancake. Cook until the tops are covered with bubbles. Flip and continue cooking until the bottoms are golden brown. Repeat process with remaining batter.

Makes about fifteen 4-inch pancakes, enough for 2

Chandler:
I'm gonna go to the bathroom. Will you watch my phone?

Monica:
Why don't you take it with you?

Chandler:
Yeah, we haven't been on a second date. She needs to hear me pee.

Lost and Found Lasagna

When Rachel's engagement ring gets lost in one of the lasagnas she's helped Monica make, Monica hesitates to mess up the food. "Oh, but look how straight those noodles are," says Rachel, admiring her handiwork. With Chandler leading the charge, they dig in to feel for the elusive bauble. Too bad this lasagna with sausage and ricotta was sacrificed in the search.

3	tablespoons olive oil
1	small onion, minced
1	medium carrot, minced
1	rib celery, minced
1½	pounds sweet Italian sausage
3½	cups canned crushed tomatoes
1	teaspoon dried oregano
1	teaspoon salt
½	teaspoon ground black pepper
18	dried lasagna noodles
2	cups ricotta cheese
¼	cup warm water
1¼	cups grated Parmesan cheese

▶ Heat the oil in a large saucepan. Add the onion and cook over medium heat until soft, about 5 minutes. Add the carrot and celery and cook until soft, about 5 minutes more. Raise the heat to medium-high, squeeze the sausage meat from its casings, and use a fork to break it into small pieces. Cook until the meat is browned, about 6 minutes. Add the tomatoes, oregano, salt, and pepper and simmer until the sauce thickens, about 20 minutes.

▶ While the sauce is simmering, cook the lasagna noodles in salted boiling water until almost al dente. Drain, refresh in a bowl of cold water, and drain again. Lay the noodles out on kitchen towels to soak up excess moisture. Stir the ricotta and warm water until smooth and set the mixture aside.

▶ Preheat the oven to 400°. Grease a 13x9-inch baking dish. Smear several tablespoons of tomato sauce (without large chunks of sausage) across the bottom of the pan. Line the pan with a layer of pasta, making sure that the noodles touch but do not overlap. Use a spatula to cover the pasta with ⅓ cup ricotta mixture. Spread 1 cup tomato sauce mixture evenly over the ricotta and then sprinkle with 3 tablespoons Parmesan. Repeat layering of the ricotta, tomato sauce, and Parmesan 5 more times, making sure to keep track of your jewelry at all times.

▶ Bake until the cheese on top turns golden brown in spots and the sauce is bubbling, 20 to 25 minutes. Remove the pan from the oven, let the lasagna settle for 5 minutes, and cut it into squares.

Serves 8

Rachel:
Remember when we were in high school together? I mean, didn't you think you were just going to meet someone and fall in love and that'd be it? Ross?

Ross:
Yes. Yes.

Rachel:
I never thought I'd be here.

Ross:
Me neither.

Italian Omelet with Spinach and Parmesan

The Italians have the right idea when it comes to making an omelet. Their version, which is called a frittata, does not involve any fancy flipping or folding of the eggs. (Leave it to the French to make eggs difficult.) Just pour the eggs and seasonings into the pan and cook until they set on the bottom. Finish cooking the top under the broiler.

6	**large eggs**
¼	**cup grated Parmesan cheese**
I	**teaspoon salt**
½	**teaspoon ground black pepper**
2	**tablespoons olive oil**
2	**medium garlic cloves, minced**
I	**10-ounce package frozen chopped spinach, thawed and squeezed dry**

▶ Beat the eggs in a medium bowl with the cheese, salt, and pepper. Set the eggs aside. Heat the oil in a large nonstick skillet. Add the garlic and sauté over medium heat until golden, about 2 minutes. Add the spinach and cook until any liquid that it throws off has evaporated, about 4 minutes.

▶ Preheat the broiler. Pour the egg mixture into the pan with the spinach and cook until the frittata is almost set, about 5 minutes. Slide the skillet under the broiler and cook until the frittata is firmly set and the top is browned, no more than 1 or 2 minutes, so pay close attention. Cut the frittata into wedges and serve.

Serves 2

Oatmeal in the Buff

When Joey tells the gang he likes to cook naked, no one quite knows what to say. "Toast. Oatmeal. Nothing that spatters," he explains. Give it a try if you dare. But hey, close the blinds first, would ya?

I ¾	**cups water**
	Pinch of salt
I	**cup old-fashioned rolled oats**
2	**tablespoons maple syrup or more for table**
	Heavy cream (at least I tablespoon per serving)

▶ Place the water, salt, and oats in a small saucepan. Bring the mixture to a boil and cook, stirring often, until the oatmeal thickens and becomes creamy, about 5 minutes. Divide the oatmeal between 2 bowls. Drizzle 1 tablespoon maple syrup over each portion. (Use more syrup if you have a real sweet tooth.) Pour a tablespoon or so of cream over each portion and serve immediately with more cream, if you like.

Serves 2

 FRITTATA
An open-faced omelet, often cooked with meat, cheese, or vegetables. Italian, from *friggere*, to fry.

The Essential Pantry

Keep these items on hand at all times, in case your neighbors from across the hall need to borrow something—again.

Baking chocolate	Nuts
Baking powder	Olive oil
Baking soda	Pasta
Barbecue sauce	Rice
Bouillon	Salad dressings
Chicken broth	Shortening
Cocoa powder	Soups
Cornstarch	Soy sauce
Evaporated milk	Spices
Flour	Sugars
Gelatin (flavored and plain)	Sweetened condensed milk
Garlic	Tabasco
Honey	Tomato paste
Infused oils and vinegars	Tomato sauce
Ketchup	Tuna
Lemon juice	Vanilla extract
Mayonnaise	Vegetable oil
Mustard (dry and prepared)	Vinegars
Nonstick cooking spray	Worcestershire sauce

Alan:
Wow . . .

Monica:
I'm really sorry.

Alan:
*I'm . . . really sorry, too.
But I've got to tell you,
I'm a little relieved.*

Monica:
Relieved?

Alan:
*Yeah, well . . . I had a
great time with you . . . I
just can't stand your
friends.*

Monica's Meat Lasagna

One bite of this dish and Aunt Syl's request for vegetarian lasagna will be forgotten. Little herbed meatballs, plenty of old-fashioned tomato sauce, and two kinds of cheese make this the ultimate comfort food.

Herbed Meatballs

I	**pound ground beef**
2	**large eggs, lightly beaten**
⅓	**cup minced fresh basil or parsley leaves**
½	**cup grated Parmesan or Pecorino Romano cheese**
½	**cup plain bread crumbs**
I½	**teaspoons salt**
½	**teaspoon ground black pepper**
	Olive oil for frying meatballs

Lasagna

3	**cups favorite tomato sauce**
18	**dried lasagna noodles**
I	**pound mozzarella cheese, shredded**
I	**cup grated Parmesan or Pecorino Romano cheese**

▶ Mix the beef, eggs, basil, cheese, bread crumbs, salt, and pepper in a large bowl with your hands until well blended. Heat about ¼ inch oil in a large skillet. Take a handful of the meatball mixture and, working directly over the skillet, pinch off pieces no larger than a small grape. Carefully drop them into the hot oil. Add as many meatballs as will fit comfortably in a single layer. Fry the meatballs, turning once or twice, until nicely browned, about 4 minutes. Use a slotted spoon to transfer cooked meatballs to a platter lined with paper towels. Repeat, adding more oil as needed, until all of the meatball mixture has been cooked.

▶ Add the meatballs to the tomato sauce and heat through for several minutes to blend flavors.

▶ Cook the pasta in salted boiling water until almost al dente. Drain, refresh in a bowl of cold water, and drain again. Lay the noodles out on kitchen towels to soak up excess moisture.

▶ Preheat the oven to 400°. Grease a 13x9-inch baking dish. Smear several tablespoons of tomato sauce (without large meatballs) across the bottom of the pan. Line the pan with a layer of pasta, making sure that the noodles touch but do not overlap. Spread ¾ cup meatballs and tomato sauce mixture evenly over the pasta. Sprinkle evenly with ⅔ cup mozzarella and 2½ tablespoons Parmesan. Repeat layering of the pasta, tomato sauce and meatballs, and cheeses four more times. For the sixth and final layer, cover the pasta with the remaining 1 cup mozzarella and then sprinkle with the remaining 3½ table-spoons Parmesan.

▶ Bake until the cheese on top turns golden brown in spots and the sauce is bubbling, 20 to 25 minutes. Remove the pan from the oven, let the lasagna settle for 5 minutes, and cut into squares.

Serves 8

Chocolate Waffle Sundaes

Marcel certainly has the right idea about waffles when he scarfs Mr. Heckles's from the hall. In this version, thick Belgian waffles are spiked with chocolate and then topped with a scoop of ice cream.

4	**tablespoons (½ stick) unsalted butter**
2	**ounces unsweetened chocolate**
½	**cup flour**
½	**teaspoon baking powder**
¼	**teaspoon salt**
½	**cup sugar**
2	**large eggs**
I	**teaspoon vanilla extract**
2	**tablespoons milk**
	Nonstick vegetable oil spray
I	**pint chocolate or vanilla ice cream**

▶ Plug in and preheat the waffle iron. Melt the butter and chocolate together in the top of a double boiler or in a microwave, stirring occasionally until smooth. Set the mixture aside to cool slightly.

▶ Stir the flour, baking powder, and salt together in a small bowl and set it aside.

▶ Beat the sugar, eggs, and vanilla together in a large bowl. Stir in the cooled chocolate mixture. Fold in the dry ingredients, alternating with a tablespoon of milk at a time, until the batter is smooth. Do not overbeat.

▶ Lightly grease the waffle iron grids with vegetable oil spray. Pour ½ cup batter over grids. (Use more for large grids.)

Close the waffle iron and cook until the waffle is well done, 3 to 4 minutes.

▶ Remove the waffle from the iron and top with ice cream. Repeat the process with the remaining batter. (You'll be too busy licking up the ice cream as it melts over the first hot waffle. So ask someone else to man the iron.)

Serves 4

"**U**gly Naked Guy's got gravity boots!"

Mr. Heckles:
I left a Belgian waffle out here. Did you take it?

Monica:
No.

Phoebe:
Why would you leave your Belgian waffle in the hall?

Mr. Heckles:
I wasn't ready for it.

Monica:
The monkey? Have you seen a monkey?

Mr. Heckles:
I saw Regis Philbin once.

Phoebe:
Okay, thank you, Mr. Heckles.

Mr. Heckles:
You owe me a waffle.

Pasta and Bean Soup

Nothing quite revives the mind and body like a bowl of hot soup. (Maybe it's the spoon thing.) This classic Italian version, called *pasta e fagioli* in Italy or "pasta fazool" in New York, is reminiscent of the sturdy cooking of Tuscany. The pasta cooks directly in an aromatic tomato broth flavored with garlic and rosemary.

¼ **cup olive oil, plus more for drizzling over bowls of soup**

4 **large cloves garlic, minced**

2 **teaspoons fresh rosemary or I teaspoon dried**

I ½ **cups canned whole tomatoes, chopped**
   Salt and ground black pepper

7 **cups chicken stock or cold water**

6 **ounces small pasta shape, such as elbows or tiny shells**

2 **19-ounce cans cannellini beans, drained and rinsed**

▶ Heat the oil in a large soup kettle or stock pot. Add the garlic and rosemary and sauté over medium heat until the garlic is golden, about 2 minutes. Add the tomatoes and a generous amount of salt and pepper to the pot. Simmer for several minutes or until the tomatoes soften.

▶ Add the chicken stock or water to the pot and bring the liquid to a boil. Reduce the heat slightly and simmer the broth briskly for 5 minutes. Add the pasta to the simmering broth and cook until the pasta is almost tender, 7 to 10 minutes, depending on the shape.

▶ Add the cooked beans to the pot and simmer for several minutes to blend flavors and finish cooking the pasta. Adjust the seasonings. Ladle hot soup into warm bowls and drizzle with olive oil to taste.

Serves 6

"**O**kay, I don't know. You . . . you just . . . have a quality."

Flirting with Firemen
Firehouse Chili

As Monica, Rachel, and Phoebe gather on Valentine's Day to burn mementos of their old boyfriends, things get out of control when Rachel throws some grappa (a high-proof Italian liqueur leftover from her Paolo period) on the flame. Next time those three will know to have some of this chili, filled with red beans, simmering on the stove before they call for help.

3	tablespoons vegetable oil
4	medium onions, chopped (be prepared with some tissues)
3	medium cloves garlic, minced
1½	pounds lean ground beef
2	cups canned crushed tomatoes
1	15-ounce can beef broth
3	tablespoons chili powder
1½	teaspoons ground cumin
½	teaspoon dried oregano
1	teaspoon salt
1	15-ounce can kidney beans, drained and rinsed

▶ Heat the oil in a large pot. Add the onions and cook over medium heat until quite soft, about 8 minutes. (The kitchen will fill up with stinging onion air, so turn on the fan if you have one.) Add the garlic and continue cooking for another 2 minutes. Stir in the ground beef and cook, using a fork to break the meat into small pieces, just until it loses its raw color, about 4 minutes.

▶ Add the tomatoes, beef broth, chili powder, cumin, oregano,

and salt. Bring the liquid to a boil, reduce the heat, and simmer gently until the liquid in the pan thickens and the flavors are nicely blended, about 2 hours. Stir in the beans and adjust the seasonings.

▶ Ladle the chili into mugs or bowls and serve with corn muffins and beer. This is the best way to beat the winter blues and makes a great Sunday meal while watching football.

Serves 6

"**U**gly Naked Guy lit a bunch of candles."

Fireman Dave:
This isn't the first boyfriend bonfire that we've seen get out of control.

Fireman Ed:
You're our third call tonight.

Phoebe:
Really?

Fireman Charlie:
Oh, sure. Valentine's is our busiest night of the year.

Festive and Holiday Selections

Complete menus for happy occasions

Monica:
Okay, we've got the coleslaw, we've got the buns. . . .

Phoebe:
We've got the ground-up flesh of formerly cute cows and turkeys.

Chandler:
Men are here.

Joey:
We make fire. Cook meat.

Chandler:
Then put out fire by peeing. No get invited back.

Rachel's Birthday Barbecue for Six

Move out onto the fire escape (or into the back yard)! This summer menu would also be a good way to celebrate the Fourth of July. Add cold beers, wine, and a juicy watermelon to round out the meal.

Clams on the Grill

Joey's Best Grilled Burgers

Creamy Coleslaw

New Potato Salad

Grilled Corn with Chili Powder (page 84)

Blueberry Cobbler (page 118)

Clams on the Grill

Shellfish taste great when cooked over hot coals. In this recipe, the clams are placed in their shells right over the flames. When they open up, squirt in a little barbecue sauce for an easy appetizer.

| 1 | cup favorite barbecue sauce (the spicier the better) |
| 24 | good-sized cherrystone or littleneck clams, scrubbed well |

▶ Light the grill. Heat the barbecue sauce on top of the stove or in a microwave. Cover and keep the sauce warm.

▶ When the fire is good and hot, place the clams on the grill. Cook until they open, 3 to 5 minutes. Use a pair of long-handled tongs to transfer the clams to a serving platter. Wearing an oven mitt, remove and discard the top shells from the clams. Spoon, squirt, or dollop a little warm barbecue

sauce into each bottom shell. By the time you have sauced all 24 clams, they should have cooled enough to serve on the half shell to guests.

Serves 6

Joey's Best Grilled Burgers

Joey might not be much of a cook, but he does know how to make a burger. After all, if Joey's anything, he's a real man's man. The Worcestershire sauce is his secret.

2	pounds ground beef
1	tablespoon Worcestershire sauce
½	teaspoon salt
½	teaspoon ground black pepper
6	buns, split

▶ Light the grill. (These burgers can be broiled or pan-fried, but they won't taste the same as meat cooked outdoors.) Gently mix the beef, Worcestershire sauce, salt, and pepper with your hands. Form the mixture into 6 patties, each about an inch thick.

▶ When the grill is hot, toast the buns (if desired), and set them aside. Grill the burgers, turning them once, until cooked as desired, about 8 minutes for medium-rare and 10 minutes for medium. Slide grilled burgers onto buns and eat at once with fixings.

Serves 6

Creamy Coleslaw

What's a cookout without coleslaw? Even citified yuppies don't break that rule.

1½	pounds green cabbage, shredded fine with a knife or in a food processor
3	medium carrots, peeled and shredded
¾	cup sour cream
1	tablespoon finely minced onion
1	teaspoon celery seed
	Salt and ground black pepper

▶ Place the shredded cabbage and carrots in a large serving bowl and chill for at least 1 hour. Stir the sour cream, onion, celery seed, and salt and pepper to taste together in a small bowl. Refrigerate the dressing. Just before serving, toss the dressing and shredded vegetables. Adjust the seasonings and serve pretty darn fast unless you like your coleslaw limp and watery.

Serves 6

"Set another place for Thanksgiving. My entire family thinks I have V.D."

New Potato Salad

Potato salad is just as important as coleslaw for a successful barbecue. This French-style recipe, with its mustard and herb dressing, is a winner.

2	pounds new potatoes, washed well
3	tablespoons white wine vinegar
1	tablespoon Dijon mustard
1	teaspoon salt
½	teaspoon ground black pepper
½	cup olive oil
2	tablespoons minced fresh chives
2	tablespoons minced fresh parsley leaves

▶ Place the unpeeled potatoes in a medium pot. Add water to cover and bring to a boil. Simmer until the potatoes are tender when pierced with a long skewer, about 15 minutes. Do not let the potatoes become mushy or soft. Drain the potatoes and set them aside to cool slightly.

▶ Meanwhile, whisk the vinegar, mustard, salt, and pepper together in a small bowl. Whisk in the oil until the dressing is smooth. Cut the slightly warm potatoes into ¼-inch-thick slices. Toss the potato slices, dressing, and fresh herbs in a large serving bowl. Mix well and adjust seasonings. Refrigerate potato salad for at least 2 hours or overnight.

Serves 6

Monica:
Hey, great skirt. Birthday present?

Rachel:
Yeah.

Monica:
From who?

Rachel:
From you. I exchanged the blouse you got me.

Chandler:
*I'd like to propose a toast.
Little toast here. I know
this isn't the Thanksgiving
any of you planned. But
for me, this has really
been great, mostly because
it didn't involve divorce or
projectile vomiting.
Anyway, I was just
thinking, if you were in
Vail, or if you were with
your families, or if you
didn't have syphilis and
stuff, we wouldn't be all
together. So I guess what
I'm trying to say is, I'm
really thankful all of your
Thanksgivings sucked.*

Ross:
*Hey, here's to a lousy
Christmas!*

Rachel:
And a crappy New Year!

Thanksgiving Dinner for Eight

This foolproof meal is a lot better than the grilled cheese sandwiches the gang eats after they burn everything on their first Thanksgiving together. With its creamy butternut squash purée, this menu also avoids that thorny issue of whose potato recipe should be served. No tater tots, lumpy mashed potatoes, or whipped potatoes with onions and peas here.

Mushroom-Barley Soup
Roast Turkey with Giblet Gravy
Cornbread Stuffing with Apples and Pecans
Cranberry-Orange Relish
Spiced Butternut Squash Purée
Shredded Brussels Sprouts with Bacon
Apple Crisp (page 115)

Mushroom-Barley Soup

Porcini are especially flavorful dried Italian mushrooms. While the mushrooms (which are sold in gourmet stores and some supermarkets) are soaking in warm water, prepare the soup base by sautéing carrots, onions, celery, and fresh mushrooms. The dried mushrooms and their richly flavored soaking liquid are then added to the aromatic vegetables. A handful of barley cooks in the soup and gives it some heft.

2   **ounces dried porcini mushrooms**
3½   **cups hot tap water**
¼   **cup olive oil**
1   **medium onion, chopped**
2   **medium carrots, diced**
2   **ribs celery, diced**
1   **pound fresh white mushrooms, sliced thin**
     Salt and ground black pepper
4   **cups chicken stock, vegetable stock, or cold water**
½   **cup barley**
¼   **cup minced fresh Italian parsley leaves**

▶ Place the porcini mushrooms in a medium bowl and cover with hot water. Soak for 20 minutes. Lift the mushrooms from the liquid with a slotted spoon and chop. Strain the soaking liquid through a colander lined with paper towels. Reserve the mushrooms and strained soaking liquid separately.

▶ While the porcini mushrooms are soaking, heat the oil in a large soup kettle or stock pot. Add the onion, carrots, and celery and sauté over medium heat until softened slightly, about 5 minutes. Add the sliced fresh mushrooms and raise the heat to medium-high. Cook, stirring often, until the mushrooms throw off their liquid, about 6 minutes. Season the vegetables generously with salt and pepper to taste.

▶ Add the porcini mushrooms, the porcini soaking liquid, and the stock or water to the pot. Bring the soup to a boil and simmer for 5 minutes to combine flavors. Stir in the barley and simmer, stirring occasionally, until the barley is tender, about 45 minutes. Stir in the parsley and adjust the seasonings. (The soup can be covered and refrigerated overnight.) Ladle hot soup into bowls or a fancy tureen.

Serves 8 as a first course

Roast Turkey with Giblet Gravy

A twelve-pound bird is more than enough for eight people for dinner with leftovers for sandwiches the next day. However, feel free to cook a larger bird if you want lots of leftovers. Of course, the cooking time should be increased when roasting a big bird.

1	**12-pound turkey, giblets and neck reserved**
5	**cups cold water**
1	**medium onion, chopped**
1	**bay leaf**
	Salt and ground black pepper
3	**tablespoons unsalted butter, melted**
2	**tablespoons cornstarch**
1	**cup white wine**
1	**teaspoon dried tarragon**

► It's easier to start the gravy early in the day or even the night before. Of course, you can do this while the turkey is roasting, but you have enough to keep you busy on Thanksgiving. Start by placing the giblets (everything in that little paper bag, minus the bag) and neck in a medium saucepan. Add the cold water, onion, and bay leaf. Simmer, skimming foam from the surface, for 1 hour. Strain the broth, discarding the vegetables and reserving the neck and giblets. When cool, remove the meat from the neck. Chop the meat and giblets and add them to the strained broth. (You can do all of this the day before cooking the turkey.)

► About 3 hours before you want to sit down, preheat the oven to 400°. Rinse and dry the turkey well. Salt and pepper the bird well. Fill the cavity with stuffing (see p. 62, or use your own recipe). Brush the skin with a little melted butter. Set the turkey, breast side down, on a rack in a large roasting pan. Place the pan in the oven and roast for 1 hour. Remove the pan from the oven, flip the bird carefully (use paper towels to get a good grip) so that the breast is facing up, and baste with more melted butter. Continue roasting and basting occasionally until meat thermometer (this is really quite necessary) stuck in the leg/thigh registers 175° to 180°, about 1½ hours longer. Transfer the turkey to a platter and let rest for 20 minutes before carving.

► Meanwhile, when the turkey is almost done, bring the reserved broth and giblets to a boil in a clean medium saucepan. Stir the cornstarch into the wine until dissolved. Add this mixture and the tarragon to the broth and simmer until the gravy thickens, about 15 minutes. When the turkey comes out of the oven, pour off the pan juices and add them to the gravy. Add salt and pepper to taste. Continue cooking the gravy over low heat until ready to sit down. Serve in a gravy boat (what else?) with sliced turkey.

Serves 8, with leftovers unless your crowd is ravenous

Monica:
Okay, looking good. Okay, cider's mulling. Turkey's turking. Yams are yamming . . . . What?

Ross:
I don't know. It's just not the same without Mom in the kitchen.

Monica:
All right, that's it. Just get out of my way and stop annoying me.

Ross:
That's closer.

Cornbread Stuffing with Apples and Pecans

What's Thanksgiving without stuffing? This version is made without meat so that any vegetarians at your table can fill up on the extra stuffing that cooks in a covered dish in the oven.

12	tablespoons (1 ½ sticks) unsalted butter
3	medium onions, chopped
2	ribs celery, chopped
3	medium Granny Smith apples, cored and chopped with peels on
6	cups cornbread (either homemade or store-bought), crumbled
3	cups white bread, crumbled
3	cups whole-wheat bread, crumbled
2	cups chopped pecans
½	cup minced fresh parsley leaves
	Salt and ground black pepper

► Melt 6 tablespoons butter in a large skillet. Add the onions and celery and cook over medium heat until the vegetables are soft and the onion becomes golden, about 10 minutes. Scrape the vegetables into a large mixing bowl.

► Melt the remaining 6 tablespoons butter in the empty pan. Add the apples and cook over medium heat until tender but not mushy, about 5 minutes. Scrape the apples into the bowl with the onions and celery. Add the crumbled breads, pecans, and parsley to the bowl and mix well. Add salt and pepper to taste.

► Place as much stuffing as will fit comfortably in the turkey cavity. Place the remaining stuffing in a buttered baking dish. Cover the dish with a piece of buttered foil and bake until the stuffing is hot. Remove the foil and let the top become crisp, if desired.

Serves 8, with some leftovers

Cranberry-Orange Relish

Instead of the usual cranberry sauce, try this raw relish that can be made in a flash in a food processor or blender.

1	pound fresh cranberries
1	medium seedless orange, quartered with peel still attached
	Sugar to taste (at least 1 cup)

► Place the cranberries and the quartered orange in the work bowl of a large food processor. (If using a blender, do this in batches.) Process, scraping down the sides as needed, until the fruit is finely ground. Scrape the relish into a large bowl. Stir in 1 cup sugar. Taste and add more sugar as desired. (If you have a sweet tooth, you might want to add as much as another cup.) Cover and refrigerate relish overnight to allow flavors to blend. (The relish can be made up to 3 days before Thanksgiving.)

Makes enough relish for Thanksgiving and days to come

Spiced Butternut Squash Purée

This creamy purée takes the place of potatoes in this menu. Of course, you could serve plain old mashed spuds (lumpy or smooth, depending on your childhood). However, this spicy purée can be made in advance, is much more interesting, and is less likely to cause friction among your friends.

2	medium butternut squash (about 4 pounds total)
4	tablespoons (½ stick) unsalted butter, cut into pieces
½	teaspoon ground cardamom
1 or 2	jalapeño peppers, stemmed and minced
2	tablespoons maple syrup
	Salt

▶ Preheat the oven to 400°. Halve the squash lengthwise and scoop out and discard the stringy pulp and seeds. Place the squash halves, cut side down, on a large baking sheet. Bake until the squash is tender, 45 minutes to 1 hour. Remove the pan from the oven and cool the squash slightly.

▶ Peel the warm squash and break the pulp into pieces. Place the squash pulp in the work bowl of a food processor. Add the butter, cardamom, peppers, maple syrup, and salt to taste. Purée, scraping down the sides as needed, until smooth. Scrape the squash purée into an ovenproof serving dish (a white casserole or large soufflé

dish is best). Cover the dish with foil. (The purée can be refrigerated overnight, if desired.)

▶ After the turkey comes out of the oven, simply pop the covered dish into the hot oven to reheat the squash purée. Serve hot.

Serves 8

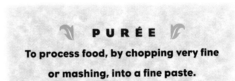

P U R É E

To process food, by chopping very fine or mashing, into a fine paste.

Monica:
You . . . you whipped the potatoes? Ross needs the lumps.

Phoebe:
Oh, I'm sorry. I just . . . I thought we could have them whipped, and then add some peas and onions.

Monica:
Why would we want to do that?

Phoebe:
Well, then they'd be just like the kind my mom used to make. Y'know, before she died.

Monica:
Ooookay . . . Three kinds of potatoes, coming up.

Shredded Brussels Sprouts with Bacon

Even people who say they don't like this holiday vegetable will love Brussels sprouts cooked with bacon and onions. (We promise!)

2	pounds Brussels sprouts
6	strips bacon
2	medium onions, chopped
	Salt and ground black pepper

► Trim the ends of the stems from the Brussels sprouts and discard any discolored leaves. Bring 1 cup of water to a boil in a large skillet with a lid. Add the trimmed sprouts, cover, and simmer over medium-low heat until tender, about 10 minutes. Drain the Brussels sprouts and set them aside to cool slightly. Shred the sprouts crosswise by slicing them with a knife. Set the sprouts aside.

► Fry the bacon in a large skillet. Transfer the strips when crisp to paper towels and drain off all but 2 tablespoons of the bacon drippings. Add the onion and cook over medium heat until tender, about 7 minutes. Add the shredded sprouts to the pan and toss well to coat them with the drippings and onions. Cook until the sprouts are heated through, about 3 minutes. Crumble the bacon slices over the pan and mix well. Add salt (sparingly) and pepper to taste. Serve immediately.

Serves 8

"Underdog has *gotten away."*

Hanukkah Dinner for Six

The eight nights of Hanukkah are celebrated by the lighting of the candles each evening and eating hearty but simple dinners like this one.

Potato Pancakes
Beef Brisket with Roasted Vegetables
Sour Cream Cake with Cinnamon Swirl

Potato Pancakes

This Eastern European dish is a favorite around the holidays. Serve with applesauce or sour cream as an appetizer or first course.

2½	pounds baking potatoes (about 5 good-sized spuds), scrubbed clean but not peeled
1	medium onion, peeled
2	large eggs, lightly beaten
¼	cup flour or matzoh meal
1	teaspoon salt
¼	teaspoon ground white pepper
	Vegetable oil for cooking the pancakes
	Applesauce or sour cream

► Shred the potatoes and onion by hand or with the shredding disc on a food processor. Place the shredded vegetables in a large bowl. Stir in the eggs, flour, salt, and pepper and mix well.

▶ Heat about ¼ inch oil in a large, heavy skillet, preferably made of cast iron. When the oil is hot, ladle about ¼ cup batter for each pancake into the pan. Cook until crisp and golden brown on the bottom, about 5 minutes. Flip and continue to cook until the other side becomes golden and crisp as well.

▶ Transfer the pancakes to a platter lined with paper towels. Let the pancakes drain for a minute or so and then serve hot with either applesauce or sour cream.

Makes about 18 pancakes

Beef Brisket with Roasted Vegetables

This is the traditional main course for Hanukkah dinners. The meat becomes incredibly tender as it slow-cooks in a covered pot in the oven.

1	**tablespoon sweet paprika**
1	**tablespoon ground black pepper**
1	**first-cut (ask your butcher) beef brisket (3 to 4 pounds)**
2	**tablespoons vegetable oil**
	Salt
1	**cup red wine**
1	**15-ounce can beef broth**
4	**medium carrots, peeled and cut into I-inch lengths**
4	**medium onions, cut into wedges**

▶ Preheat the oven to 350°. Combine the paprika and pepper and rub this mixture into the brisket with your hands. Heat the oil in a large Dutch oven set over medium-high heat. Add the brisket and cook until both sides are nicely browned, about 10 minutes. Remove the brisket from the pan, season it generously with salt, and set it aside briefly.

▶ Add the wine to the pan and simmer, scraping the bottom to loosen any browned bits, for about 3 minutes. Add the beef broth and bring the liquid to a boil. Return the brisket to the pan and add the carrots and onions. Cover the pan and transfer it to the oven. Cook the brisket, turning it once and basting the meat occasionally, until it is quite tender, about 2½ hours.

▶ Transfer the brisket to a cutting board and cool slightly. Slice the meat across the grain into thin strips. Serve with roasted carrots and onions as well as the pan gravy.

Serves 6, with meat left over for sandwiches the next day

Ross:
Okay, I think it's time to change somebody's nicotine patch.

Monica:
Hey. Where's Joey?

Chandler:
Joey ate my last stick of gum, so I killed him. Do you think that was wrong?

"Chandler Bing, it's time to see your thing!**"**

Sour Cream Cake with Cinnamon Swirl

A swirl of cinnamon, pecans, and brown sugar enlivens this moist sour cream yellow cake. Serve with coffee for a fitting holiday dinner finale.

Cinnamon Swirl

⅔   cup firmly packed brown sugar

½   cup finely chopped pecans or walnuts

1½   teaspoons ground cinnamon

Sour Cream Cake

12   tablespoons (1½ sticks) unsalted butter, softened

1½   cups sugar

3   large eggs

2   teaspoons vanilla extract

3   cups flour

1½   teaspoons baking powder

1½   teaspoons baking soda

¼   teaspoon salt

1½   cups sour cream

▶ Preheat the oven to 375°. Grease a large tube pan (the kind used to make angel food cake) and set it aside. Combine the brown sugar, pecans, and cinnamon in a small bowl and set the mixture aside.

▶ Cream the butter and sugar with an electric mixer until light and fluffy, about 1 minute. Beat in the eggs, one at a time, until the batter is smooth. Beat in the vanilla.

▶ Stir the flour, baking powder, baking soda, and salt together in a medium bowl. Add the dry ingredients to the batter, alternating with the sour cream, until all the flour mixture and sour cream have been added and the batter is smooth.

▶ Pour half of the batter into the prepared pan. Sprinkle half of the nut mixture evenly over the batter. Carefully pour the remaining batter on top of the nut mixture. Sprinkle remaining nut mixture over the top of the batter. Bake until a toothpick inserted in the center of the cake comes out clean, 50 to 55 minutes. Cool the cake in the pan on a rack. Remove the cake from the pan and cut it into wedges.

Serves 6, with enough for the next night if the cake lasts that long

Christmas Tree Trimming Party for Twelve

Gather your own friends for an old-fashioned celebration. Greet them at the door with bar nuts and olives. When things move into high gear, serve savory pies, salad, and bread all on one plate that revelers can keep on their laps, along with a fork and napkin. Finish up with a selection of holiday cookies and egg nog.

Roasted Bar Nuts with Rosemary (page 10)

Marinated Spanish Olives with Garlic and Herbs (page 11)

Spinach Savory Pie

Bacon and Mushroom Savory Pie

Italian Tri-Color Salad with Balsamic Vinaigrette

Assortment of Store-Bought Breads

Holiday Egg Nog

Jamie and Fran's Chocolate Biscotti (page 23)

Pine Nut Cookies (page 32)

Orange Shortbread (page 18)

Spinach Savory Pie

Real men may not eat quiche, but if you call it a savory pie who will know the difference?

I	**9-inch pie crust (use a frozen crust, if desired)**
2	**tablespoons unsalted butter**
I	**small onion, minced**
I	**10-ounce package fresh spinach, stemmed and washed**
I	**teaspoon salt**
¼	**teaspoon ground black pepper**
3	**large eggs**
¾	**cup milk**
⅓	**cup shredded Swiss cheese**

▶ Preheat the oven to 400°. Prick the bottom of the crust with a fork. Bake the crust until it just starts to color, 10 to 12 minutes. Remove the crust from the oven and set it aside. Lower the oven to 375°.

▶ While the crust is in the oven, melt the butter in a large pot. Add the onion and cook over medium heat until soft, about 5 minutes. Chop the damp spinach and add it to the pan. Cover and cook, stirring occasionally, until the spinach is tender, about 5 minutes. Drain off any liquid in the pot and season with salt and pepper.

▶ Whisk the eggs and milk together in a large bowl. Stir in the spinach mixture and cheese. Pour the entire mixture into the prebaked pie crust. Place the pie tin on a baking sheet and slide it into the oven. Bake until the pie puffs and the top is golden brown, 35 to 40 minutes. Let the pie settle for at least 10 minutes before cutting it into wedges. (This savory pie can be cooled completely, covered with foil, and then reheated later in the day, if desired.)

Serves 6

Monica:
So, how'd it go?

Joey:
I didn't get the job.

Ross:
How could you not get it? You were Santa last year.

Joey:
I don't know. Some fat guy's sleeping with the store manager. He's not even jolly. It's all political.

Monica:
So, what are you gonna be?

Joey:
I'm one of his helpers. It's just such a slap in the face.

Monica:
Mom already called this morning. Just to remind me not to wear my hair up. Did you know my ears are not my best feature?

Ross:
Some days it's all I can think about.

"Ugly Naked Guy got a Thighmaster."

Bacon and Mushroom Savory Pie

Meat eaters will love this hearty quiche, which is the perfect complement to Spinach Savory Pie.

1	**9-inch pie crust (use a frozen crust if desired)**
6	**strips bacon**
1	**small onion, minced**
6	**ounces fresh white mushrooms, sliced thin**
	Salt and ground black pepper
3	**large eggs**
¾	**cup milk**
½	**cup shredded Cheddar cheese**

► Preheat the oven to 400°. Prick the bottom of the crust with a fork. Bake the crust until it just starts to color, 10 to 12 minutes. Remove the crust from the oven and set it aside. Lower the temperature to 375°.

► While the crust is in the oven, fry the bacon in a large skillet until crisp. Transfer the bacon to a plate lined with paper towels and set it aside. Pour off all but 1 tablespoon of the bacon drippings. Add the onion and cook over medium heat until soft, about 5 minutes. Add the mushrooms and cook until they are golden and considerably shrunken, about 8 minutes. Drain off any liquid in the pot. Crumble the bacon and stir it into the pot. Season with salt and pepper to taste.

► Whisk the eggs and milk together in a large bowl. Stir in the mushroom-bacon mixture and cheese. Pour the entire mixture into the prebaked pie crust. Place the pie tin on a baking sheet and slide it into the oven. Bake until the pie puffs and the top is golden brown, about 35 minutes. Let the pie settle for at least 10 minutes before cutting it into wedges. (This savory pie can be cooled completely, covered with foil, and then reheated later in the day, if desired.)

Serves 6

"I can't even get Marcel to stop eating the bathmat. How am I going to raise a kid?"

Mushroom Mania

Specialty mushroom sales are booming, according to the U.S. Department of Agriculture. Here are a few to consider the next time you're cruising the aisles of your local market.

Button: Probably the most available mushroom, these are also known as "whites." Raw buttons have a mild, delicate flavor, which is retained in cooking. These can be sautéed, grilled, or marinated, and are good for stuffings, salads, kabobs, and appetizers.

Cremini: Close in appearance to buttons, cremini mushrooms have a meaty texture and earthy flavor. They can be sautéed, grilled, or marinated for a variety of uses, and are good in soups and stews.

Enoki: These mushrooms have long, thin stems, somewhat resembling bean sprouts. Their subtle, earthy flavor is great for salads and garnishes.

Morel: Biting into a morel gives you a nutty taste. Cooking them will make them somewhat chewy, so think about adding them to cream sauces or sautéing them for serving over meats.

Oyster: One look at these mushrooms and you will indeed be reminded of an oyster. Cooking these delicately flavored mushrooms will give them a velvety texture. Sauté or grill these mushrooms for chicken, soups, or fish.

Portobello: These wide-topped mushrooms have a meaty flavor and texture when cooked. Their size makes them great grilled or baked for an appetizer, or even sautéed as a light entrée.

Shiitake: You find these mushrooms on a lot of restaurant menus, especially in omelets or on pizzas. They have a woodsy flavor and meaty texture when cooked. Chances are you'll either love 'em or hate 'em.

Ross:
Hey, Joey, are you okay?

Joey:
Yeah, I guess. It's just, you know, they're parents. After a certain point, you gotta let go. Even if you know better, you gotta let them make their own mistakes.

Rachel:
And just think, in a couple of years, we get to turn into them.

Chandler:
If I turn into my parents, I'll either be an alcoholic blonde chasing twenty-year-old boys, or . . . I'll wind up like my mom.

Italian Tri-Color Salad with Balsamic Vinaigrette

Endive, arugula, and radicchio are the three colorful components in a classic Italian salad. Add some soft leaf lettuce to mellow out these slightly bitter greens.

2	medium heads Belgian endive
2	large heads radicchio
1	large bunch arugula
2	large heads red leaf lettuce
1½	tablespoons balsamic vinegar
1½	tablespoons red wine vinegar
	Salt and ground black pepper
½	cup olive oil

▶ Wash and dry the salad greens. Tear them into bite-sized pieces and place them in a large salad bowl. (Cover with plastic wrap and refrigerate for several hours, if desired.)

▶ Whisk the vinegars and salt and pepper to taste together in a small bowl. Slowly whisk in the oil until the dressing is smooth. (The dressing can be refrigerated and rewhisked just before serving, if desired.) Drizzle as much dressing as desired over the salad greens and toss gently. Serve salad immediately.

Serves 12

"Hi, Ben. Hi. I'm your Aunt Monica. I . . . I will always have gum.**"**

Holiday Egg Nog

Serve this spiced nog with the cookies for a rousing finish to your tree trimming party. If you decide to omit the alcohol, add an extra ½ cup milk.

3	cups milk
8	large eggs, lightly beaten
½	cup sugar
2	teaspoons vanilla extract
¼	cup rum, optional
¼	cup brandy, optional
1½	cups heavy cream
	Ground cinnamon
	Ground nutmeg

▶ Combine the milk, eggs, and sugar in a large, heavy saucepan. Heat the mixture over medium heat until it is thick enough to coat a spoon. Do not let the mixture come to a boil. Pour the mixture into a bowl set in a larger bowl of ice water. Stir in the vanilla, rum, and brandy. When the mixture has cooled slightly, refrigerate it until well chilled (at least several hours or overnight, if desired).

▶ When ready to party, whip the heavy cream with an electric mixer until soft peaks form. Fold the whipped cream into the chilled nog. Pour the mixture into a punch bowl and sprinkle with cinnamon and nutmeg to taste. Ladle into cups and serve immediately.

Serves 12

New Year's Eve Buffet for Fifteen to Twenty

With the exception of the greens, all of these recipes can be prepared in advance and either served at room temperature or reheated as desired. This way you get to count down the minutes until midnight with your guests, instead of slaving alone over a hot stove.

Smoked Salmon Canapés with Dill Cream Cheese (page 8)

Spiced Pecans (page 9)

Baked Ham with Sherry-Mustard Glaze

Country Herb Biscuits

Black-Eyed Peas with Onions and Tomatoes

Garlicky Winter Greens

Cranberry-Pear Pies (make two; see page 118)

Baked Ham with Sherry-Mustard Glaze

Buying a smoked ham is the smart way to go when feeding a crowd. All you need to do is bake the ham until it is heated through and then brush it with the sweet-and-spicy glaze. The ham can be served warm or at room temperature.

I	fully cooked smoked ham with the bone in (12 to 14 pounds)
I	cup apple cider
½	cup sherry
⅓	cup firmly packed brown sugar
¼	cup Dijon mustard

▶ Preheat the oven to 350°. Trim the thick rind from the ham, leaving behind a ⅛-inch-thick layer of fat. Use a sharp knife to score the ham in a diamond pattern, if desired. Line a large roasting pan with aluminum foil (this will make clean-up a lot easier) and place the ham on the foil. Pour the cider into the pan. Bake the ham for 1½ hours, basting frequently with the cider.

▶ Mix the sherry, brown sugar, and mustard together and brush the glaze over the ham. Continue baking, basting occasionally with the glaze and pan juices, until the ham is nicely browned, about 30 minutes. Remove the ham from the oven and let it rest for at least 30 minutes before carving. Serve warm or let the ham cool to room temperature and then carve.

Serves 15 to 20

Chandler:
You know that thing when you and I talk to each other about things?

Joey:
Yeah.

Chandler:
Let's not do that anymore.

Rachel:
Are you seeing her again tonight?

Joey:
Yup. Ice Capades.

Chandler:
Wow. This is serious. I've never known you to pay money for any kind of capade.

Country Herb Biscuits

Ham cries out for good country biscuits. The dill or chives in these miniature biscuits complement the glazed ham nicely.

4	**cups flour**
4	**teaspoons baking powder**
I	**teaspoon baking soda**
I	**teaspoon salt**
¼	**cup minced fresh dill or chives**
16	**tablespoons (2 sticks) chilled unsalted butter, cut into small pieces**
I ½	**cups buttermilk**

► Preheat the oven to 450°. Place the flour, baking powder, baking soda, salt, and herbs in the work bowl of a large food processor. Pulse just to combine the ingredients. Add the butter and pulse until the mixture resembles coarse crumbs. Slowly pour the buttermilk through the feed tube and pulse just until the dough comes together.

► Turn the dough out onto a floured counter. Divide the dough in half. Roll each half to a thickness of about ½ inch. Use a 1-inch cookie cutter or juice glass to punch out biscuits. Reroll scraps and punch out more biscuits.

► Place the biscuits on 2 large ungreased baking sheets, leaving about an inch between them. Bake until the tops are golden brown, about 8 minutes. Serve warm or cool to room temperature, and reheat at serving time.

Makes about 4 dozen little biscuits

Black-Eyed Peas with Onions and Tomatoes

Black-eyed peas are traditionally served at New Year's to ensure good luck during the coming year. (It couldn't hurt, could it?) This dish can be prepared in advance and then reheated at serving time. It's also delicious at room temperature.

3	**cups dried black-eyed peas**
½	**cup olive oil**
2	**medium onions, chopped**
4	**medium cloves garlic, minced**
I	**28-ounce can whole tomatoes packed in juice**
¼	**cup minced fresh parsley leaves**
	Salt and ground black pepper

► Place the peas in a large bowl and cover with cold water. Soak the peas overnight. Drain the peas and place them in a large pot. Add cold water to cover and simmer until the peas are tender, about 40 minutes. Drain the peas and set them aside.

► Heat the oil in a large saucepan. Add onion and cook until soft, about 5 minutes. Stir in the garlic and cook for another minute or two. Coarsely chop the tomatoes and add them to the pan along with their packing liquid. Simmer until the mixture thickens a bit, about 15 minutes. Stir in the black-eyed peas and parsley and cook until the peas are heated through, about 5 minutes. Add salt and pepper to taste. Serve hot, warm, or at room temperature.

Serves 15 to 20

Garlicky Winter Greens

Use spinach, beet greens, or even Swiss chard in this recipe. The greens will cook down considerably, so you will need a very large pot to hold them all.

5   **pounds spinach or other greens**
½   **cup olive oil**
8   **medium cloves garlic, minced**
     Salt and ground black pepper

▶ Remove the stems from the greens and wash the leaves thoroughly to remove all traces of sand. Leave the greens slightly damp. Heat the oil in a large kettle. Add the garlic and cook over medium heat until golden, about 2 minutes. Add the greens and stir to coat them with the oil. Cover, stirring occasionally, until the greens are tender, about 7 minutes. Season with salt and pepper to taste and serve hot.

Serves 15 to 20

JULIENNE

To cut food, usually vegetables, into thin strips, about ⅛ inch square by 1 to 2 inches long.

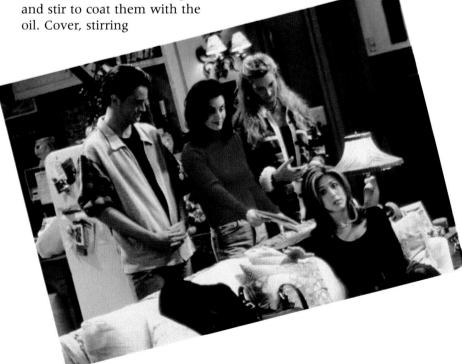

Chandler:
Yeah. I think for us, kissing is pretty much an opening act. You know. I mean, it's like . . . the comedian you have to sit through before Pink Floyd comes out.

Ross:
And it's not that we don't like the comedian. It's just . . . that's not why we bought the ticket.

Chandler:
You see, the problem is, though, after the concert's over, no matter how great the show was you girls are always looking for the comedian again. You know? I mean, we're in the car. We're fighting traffic. Basically . . . just trying to stay awake.

Rachel:
Yeah, well, word of advice: Bring back the comedian. Otherwise, next time you're going to find yourself sitting at home listening to that album alone.

Joey:
Are we still talking about sex?

Chandler:
How . . . how can I dump this woman on Valentine's Day?

Joey:
I don't know. You dumped her on New Year's.

Chandler:
Man, in my next life, I'm coming back as a toilet brush.

Romantic Valentine's Day Dinner for Two

You want to serve something special but you don't have the energy to cook for days on end. After all, you need plenty of time for personal grooming. This menu is sophisticated and sensual, and won't leave you utterly exhausted for after-dinner activities.

Chilled Jumbo Shrimp with Spicy Cocktail Sauce
Steamed Lobsters with Herb Butter
Lemon Rice Pilaf with Asparagus
Individual Chocolate Soufflés (page 120)

Chilled Jumbo Shrimp with Spicy Cocktail Sauce

Start things off with a bang. Jumbo shrimp that you can purchase cooked and peeled at the fish market are a great choice. This old-fashioned appetizer is jazzed up with home-made cocktail sauce, which can be prepared the day before the big evening.

¼   **cup ketchup**
1   **tablespoon prepared horseradish**
1   **tablespoon lemon juice**
     Tabasco or other bottled hot sauce
8   **jumbo shrimp, cooked and peeled**
     Plenty of crushed ice
     Lemon wedges

▶ Stir the ketchup, horseradish, lemon juice, and hot sauce together in a small bowl. Cover and refrigerate until well chilled. (The sauce can be refrigerated up to 3 days.)

▶ Find 2 pretty bowls (or better

yet, goblets) and fill them with crushed ice. Arrange 4 shrimp over each mound of ice and garnish with lemon wedges. Serve immediately with cocktail sauce on the side and champagne in your glasses.

Serves 2

"Smile, you're on Janice Camera."

Steamed Lobsters with Herb Butter

Nothing says "I love you" like a lobster. Be prepared to get messy. But isn't cleaning up together half the fun?

2   **live lobsters**
6   **tablespoons butter**
1   **tablespoon minced fresh tarragon, basil, or chives**
     Salt and ground black pepper

▶ Place a rack in a large pot and fill with several inches of water. (The water should still be below the rack.) Bring the water to a boil and carefully place the lobsters on the rack. Cover the pot and steam until the lobsters are fire-engine red, 10 to 12 minutes.

▶ While the lobsters are cooking, melt the butter in a small pan. Stir in the herbs and salt and pepper to taste and divide the herb butter between 2 small ramekins or dishes that have been warmed under hot tap water and dried well.

▶ Use tongs to lift the cooked lobsters onto individual plates. Serve with herb butter, nut crackers to open the shells, an empty bowl for the shells, and plenty of napkins. Chardonnay goes well with lobsters or continue with the bubbly.

Serves 2

Lemon Rice Pilaf with Asparagus

This lemony pilaf contains both starch and vegetable to round out your special meal. By the way, the Romans considered asparagus to be an aphrodisiac. (Does Chandler know about this?) Maybe they were right. It's worth a try.

2	**tablespoons olive oil**
1	**small onion, chopped**
2	**medium cloves garlic, minced**
1	**teaspoon grated lemon zest**
¼	**cup white wine**
1	**cup long-grain rice**
1½	**cups water**
½	**teaspoon salt**
¼	**pound thin asparagus spears**

▶ Heat the oil in a medium pot with a lid. Add the onion and cook over medium heat until soft, about 5 minutes. Stir in the garlic, lemon zest, and wine and cook for 1 minute. Add the rice, water, and salt. Cover the pot, reduce the heat to low, and cook until the rice is tender and fluffy, about 15 minutes.

▶ While the rice is cooking, snap the tough ends from the asparagus spears. Cut the asparagus on the bias into ¾-inch pieces. Bring several cups of water to a boil in a small pan. Add the asparagus and cook until tender, about 2 minutes. Drain the asparagus and set it aside.

▶ Stir the asparagus into the cooked rice. Adjust the seasonings. Keep the pot covered until ready to serve. The rice can be held for 15 minutes.

Serves 2

"That's a relatively open weave, and I can still see your, uh ... nippular areas."

Phoebe:
Ooo, you know my friend Abby who shaves her head? She says that if you want to break the bad boyfriend cycle, you can do, like, a cleansing ritual.

Rachel:
Pheebs ... this woman is voluntarily bald.

Phoebe:
Yeah! We can do it tomorrow night, you guys. It's Valentine's Day. It's perfect.

Monica:
Okay, well ... what kind of ritual?

Phoebe:
Okay. We can, um ... we can burn the stuff they gave us. ...

Rachel:
Or. ...

Phoebe:
Or, we can chant and dance around naked—you know, with sticks.

Monica:
Burning's good.

Rachel:
Burning's good. I got stuff to burn.

Urban Eating

Dishes inspired by city living

Ross:
Hey. When did you and Susan meet Huey Lewis?

Carol:
Uh, that's our friend Tanya.

Grilled Tuna with Ginger and Garlic

As New Yorkers like to boast, you can eat in a different country every night of the month without ever leaving the city. Japanese restaurants are among the most popular. Ross once took a date to a Japanese place. Unfortunately, Carol and Susan ended up sitting across from them and the date was a bust. This dish, however, is foolproof.

4	tuna steaks (about 8 ounces each)
3	tablespoons soy sauce
1	tablespoon dark sesame oil
1	tablespoon rice vinegar or cider vinegar
2	teaspoons minced fresh ginger root
2	medium cloves garlic, minced
1	medium scallion, sliced thin
	Ground black pepper

▶ Place the tuna steaks in a large glass or ceramic baking dish. Combine the soy sauce, sesame oil, vinegar, ginger, garlic, and scallion in a small bowl. Brush the marinade on both sides of the fish. Sprinkle the fish with pepper to taste. Cover and refrigerate the fish for 30 minutes, turning once after 15 minutes.

▶ While the fish is in the fridge, light the grill. When hot, scrape the grill surface clean. Grill the fish, turning once, until it is cooked the way you like it, about 8 minutes for medium-rare. Serve grilled fish with white rice as well as a steamed vegetable if you like.

Serves 4

Turkey on Rye with Homemade Russian

Oversized corned beef, pastrami, roast beef, tongue, and turkey sandwiches satisfy our craving for excess. Russian dressing is the condiment of choice. As for bread, how could you consider anything other than rye?

1/4	cup mayonnaise
1	tablespoon ketchup
2	teaspoons sweet pickle relish
1	teaspoon prepared horseradish
1	teaspoon Worcestershire sauce
4	slices rye bread
1/2	pound sliced turkey (from a real bird, not some pressed loaf)

▶ Mix the mayo, ketchup, relish, horseradish, and Worcestershire sauce in a small bowl. Taste and adjust to personal preferences (i.e., add more relish if you like it sweet, more horseradish if you like it hot, or more Worcestershire if you like it salty). Slather Russian dressing over each slice of bread. Pile the turkey meat high on 2 slices of bread and cover with remaining 2 slices. Cut the sandwiches in half and open wide.

Makes 2 sandwiches

Blini with Salmon Caviar and Sour Cream

This dish, with Russian-style pancakes, is a classic that will make you think you're dining at the Russian Tea Room in Manhattan. Salmon caviar is a delicious and affordable alternative to beluga caviar (unless you already have a second job).

2   **cups milk**
2   **teaspoons active dry yeast**
2   **teaspoons sugar**
1   **cup buckwheat flour**
¾   **cup regular flour**
½   **teaspoon salt**
4   **tablespoons (½ stick) butter, melted**
3   **large eggs, lightly beaten**
     Vegetable oil for cooking the blini
1   **cup sour cream**
4   **ounces salmon caviar (or more if you like)**

▶ Heat the milk in a small saucepan. When lukewarm, pour the milk into a large bowl. Stir in the yeast and sugar and let stand for 5 minutes. Stir in the flours, salt, butter, and eggs until smooth. Cover the bowl with a damp towel and let the dough rise until doubled in bulk, about 1 hour.

▶ Preheat the oven to 250°. Pour enough oil into a large nonstick skillet just to coat the bottom. When the pan is hot, ladle the batter by the tablespoon into the pan, leaving plenty of space for each blini to spread. (The technique is the same as with regular American pancakes.) When the tops are covered with bubbles, turn the blini and continue cooking until the bottoms are golden. Transfer the blini to a platter and keep warm in the oven while you cook up the rest of the batter. (You can eat blini straight from the pan if you like.) Top each blini with a dollop of sour cream and a small spoonful of caviar.

Serves 8 as an appetizer or 12 at a cocktail party

Coney Island Egg Cream

This soda fountain classic contains no eggs or cream. No doubt the name refers to the foamy head (it looks like an egg white) that forms when this beverage is correctly prepared. An old-fashioned seltzer bottle for shooting soda into the glass is essential.

2   **tablespoons chocolate syrup**
1   **cup milk**
⅓   **cup seltzer**

▶ Pour the syrup into a tall glass. Stir in the milk. Shoot the seltzer from an old-fashioned bottle directly into the glass until the foam reaches the rim. Drink immediately.

Serves 1

Rachel:
You know, it was actually really great. He took me to lunch at the Russian Tea Room. I had that chicken where you poke it and butter squirts out.

Phoebe:
Not a good day for birds.

Matt LeBlanc / JOEY

Matt LeBlanc, a native of Newton, Massachusetts, has starred in several comedy series, including *Top of the Heap, Vinnie & Bobby*, and *TV 101*. He appeared in *Anything to Survive* and guest starred on *Class of '96, The Red Shoe Diaries*, and *Just the Ten of Us*. LeBlanc served his time as a Levi's model and made his feature film debut in *Looking Italian*.

Fire Escape Flank Steak

Even though most New Yorkers live in apartments, they still like to grill, especially during muggy Manhattan summers. Thank heavens for fire escapes and balconies, like the one off Monica and Rachel's apartment.

¼	cup vegetable oil
3	tablespoons lime juice
1	tablespoon minced garlic
1	teaspoon ground cumin
1	teaspoon chili powder
1 or 2	jalapeño peppers (use as many as you can tolerate), stemmed and minced
2	tablespoons minced fresh cilantro leaves
1	flank steak (about 2 pounds), trimmed of excess fat
	Salt

▶ Whisk the oil, lime juice, garlic, cumin, chili powder, jalapeños, and cilantro together in a small bowl. Place the meat in a shallow pan. Pour or brush the marinade over meat. Cover the pan and refrigerate for at least 1 hour or overnight.

▶ Light the grill. Generously sprinkle both sides of the steak with salt to taste. Scrape the hot grill surface clean. Grill the steak, turning once, until done the way you like it, 8 to 10 minutes for medium-rare. Transfer the steak to a platter and carve, cutting meat into thin slices across the grain.

Serves 6

i

Chandler's "Could This BE Any More Fattening?" Cheesecake

The name of this New York classic says it all. The higher-then-lower cooking temperatures ensure that this version is creamy and dense.

Graham Cracker Crust

1	**cup graham cracker crumbs**
2	**tablespoons sugar**
3	**tablespoons unsalted butter, melted**

Ultimate Cheesecake

2	**pounds cream cheese**
1¼	**cups sugar**
4	**large eggs**
½	**cup sour cream**
1	**teaspoon vanilla extract**

▶ Adjust the oven rack to the middle position; preheat the oven to 450°. Combine the graham cracker crumbs, 2 tablespoons sugar, and melted butter in a small bowl. Mix well, and press crumbs into the bottom and sides of a 9-inch springform pan with your fingers.

▶ Beat the cream cheese in a large bowl until fluffy and light, about 2 minutes. Beat in the sugar until smooth. Add the eggs one at a time, beating well after each addition. Beat in the sour cream and vanilla.

▶ Pour the batter into the prepared pan. Bake for 15 minutes. Open the oven door and lower the temperature to 200°. (Make this recipe when your kitchen seems a bit chilly and drafty.) Close the oven door and continue baking until the edges of the cheesecake are set, but the center still wiggles when the pan is shaken, about 1 hour. (Remember John Travolta's hips in *Saturday Night Fever*?)

▶ Cool the cheesecake on a rack to room temperature. Refrigerate for at least 3 hours before serving. Cut into individual pieces by dipping a knife into hot water between slices.

Serves 12

Joey:
Monica, I'm telling you this guy is perfect for you!

Monica:
Forget it. Not after your cousin who could belch the alphabet.

Janice:
By the way, Chandler . . . I cut you out of all my pictures. So, if you want, I have a bag with just your heads.

Monica:
Wait. He pooped in my shoe? Which one?

Rachel:
I don't know. The left one.

Monica:
Which ones?

Rachel:
Oh . . . those little clunky, Amish things you think go with everything.

Perfect Pizza Dough

For many New Yorkers, pizza is one of the four basic food groups, along with Chinese takeout, hot dogs, and bagels. New York-style pizza has a thin crust that becomes crisp in super-hot brick ovens. Home cooks can duplicate this effect by using a ceramic pizza stone. Place the stone in the oven and heat at the highest setting (500° on most ovens) for 30 minutes. The stone absorbs heat especially well and gives the crust that slightly charred brick-oven taste. Of course, pizza made on a baking sheet in a very hot oven is also quite good.

1 ⅓ **cups warm water (105° to 115°)**

2 **teaspoons active dry yeast**

3 **tablespoons olive oil**

3 ½ **cups flour**

1 ¼ **teaspoons salt**

Cornmeal for sprinkling under dough

▶ Pour the water into the work bowl of a food processor. Add the yeast and oil and process for several seconds until smooth. Add the flour and salt and process until the dough comes together in a ball, about 30 seconds.

▶ Turn the dough into a large bowl and cover with a damp towel. Let rise until the dough is puffy and has increased in bulk by 1 ½ times, 45 minutes to 1 hour. Divide the dough in half and let each half rise, covered, in a separate medium bowl for 20 minutes. (The dough can be refrigerated in airtight containers overnight or frozen for up to 1 week. Bring to room temperature before rolling out and topping.)

▶ Working on a pizza peel or large rimless baking sheet that has been sprinkled with cornmeal, use fingertips to flatten 1 dough ball into an 8-inch disc. Slowly rotate the disc, gently stretching the dough to the side as you turn it. (You can try tossing the dough in the air, but be warned that this is harder than it looks.) When the dough is almost the right size (about 12 inches), thin the edge by flattening and stretching it with your fingertips.

▶ Top and bake pizza according to one of the recipes that follow. Repeat the process with the second dough.

Enough for two 12-inch pizzas

"Things sure have changed here on Walton's Mountain.**"**

Riff's Tuna Melt with Swiss

When Joey is smitten with Ursula, he starts hanging out at Riff's, where she works. "I went back to Riff's. I think Ursula likes me. All I ordered was coffee, but she brought me a tuna melt and four plates of curly fries." Too bad Joey didn't realize it was nothing personal.

1	**6-ounce can tuna packed in water, drained**
1	**rib celery, minced**
2	**tablespoons minced fresh parsley leaves**
	Ground black pepper
3	**tablespoons mayonnaise or to taste**
4	**slices whole-wheat bread**
4	**thin slices tomato**
4	**thin slices Swiss cheese**

▶ Break up the tuna with a fork. Stir in the celery, parsley, and pepper to taste. Stir in the mayo. Use more or less than 3 tablespoons, if you like tuna salad that is especially dry or moist.

▶ Preheat the broiler and then toast slices of bread on both sides. Lay 2 slices of bread on a small baking sheet and reserve 2 other slices. Divide the tuna salad among the 2 slices of bread on the baking sheet. Lay 2 tomato slices across each mound of tuna, followed by 2 slices of cheese.

▶ Slide the baking sheet under the broiler and cook just until the cheese melts. Remove the baking sheet from the oven and place the reserved slices of toast over the melted cheese to form sandwiches. Slice the sandwiches in half on the diagonal. Serve with curly fries, at least 4 plates.

Makes 2 sandwiches

Ross's Scrambled Eggs and Lox

If you don't have a sexy neighbor who'll loan you what you need, you'll just have to get your eggs at the market like the rest of us.

4	**large eggs**
2	**tablespoons minced fresh chives or scallions**
	Ground black pepper
2	**tablespoons butter**
2	**ounces Nova-style smoked salmon (lox), cut into ½-inch pieces**

▶ Beat the eggs with a fork or whisk until smooth. Stir in the chives and pepper to taste.

▶ Melt the butter in a large skillet set over medium heat. Add the egg mixture and stir gently with a fork or spatula until the eggs begin to set. Stir in the lox and continue cooking until the eggs are cooked the way you like them. Divide the lox and eggs between 2 plates and serve with either home fries or toasted bagels.

Serves 2

❧ LOX ❧

Salmon that has been cured with salt.

Chandler:
Come on, Ross. You got to get back in the game here, okay? The Rachel thing's not happening. Your ex-wife's a lesbian. You . . . I don't think we need a third.

Joey:
Excuse me. Could we have an egg here? Still in the shell? Thanks.

Ross:
An egg?

Joey:
Yeah, you're going to go up to her and say: "Here's your egg back. I'm returning your egg."

Chandler:
I think it's winning.

Ross:
I think it's insane.

Chandler:
She'll love it.

Joey and Chandler:
There you go. Go. Go.

Joey:
Think it'll work?

Chandler:
No way. It's suicide. The man's got an egg.

Janice:
*You seek me out.
Something deep in your
soul calls out to me like a
foghorn: "Jaaaanice . . .
Jaaaanice . . ."
You want me. You need
me. You can't live
without me. And you
know it. You just don't
know you know it. See ya.*

Janice's Foghorn Fish Dish

Even though Janice is extremely
loud, Chandler never seems to hear
her coming. Maybe he really does
love her. Or maybe not.

4	**small boneless flounder or sole fillets (about 6 ounces each)**
	Salt and ground black pepper
1	**large egg**
1	**cup plain bread crumbs**
3	**tablespoons olive oil**
3	**medium shallots, minced**
3	**medium plum tomatoes, cored and cut into ½-inch cubes**
2	**tablespoons tarragon vinegar**
2	**tablespoons minced fresh parsley leaves**

▶ Sprinkle the fish with salt and
pepper to taste. Beat the egg in a
shallow bowl. Place the bread
crumbs in another shallow bowl.
Dip the fish in the egg and then
the crumbs, turning fish until
both sides are evenly coated with
crumbs.

▶ Heat 1 tablespoon oil in a large
skillet. Add 2 fillets and cook
over medium-high heat until the
bottoms are nicely browned, 2 to
3 minutes. Turn fish and continue
cooking until browned on the
second side. Transfer cooked
fillets to a plate and cover to
keep them warm. Add another
tablespoon oil to the pan and
cook the second batch of fish.
Keep all 4 fillets warm on a plate
while making the pan sauce.

▶ Add the remaining tablespoon oil
and shallots to the pan. Cook for
2 minutes. Add the tomatoes and
salt and pepper to taste and cook
for another 2 minutes. Add the
vinegar and parsley and simmer
for 30 seconds. Adjust the
seasonings. Place each fillet on
an individual plate and spoon
some of the sauce over the fish.

Serves 4

Grilled Corn with Chili Powder

This southwestern-style grilled corn
can be made on the smallest hibachi,
often the only barbecue that will fit
on tiny apartment balconies. Cooking the naked ears right over the
flames brings out their sweetness.

2	**tablespoons chili powder**
1	**teaspoon salt**
¼	**cup corn oil**
6	**ears fresh corn, husked**

▶ Light the grill. When hot, scrape
the grill surface clean. Meanwhile,
combine the chili powder with
salt. Stir in the oil and brush the
mixture over husked ears of
corn. Grill the corn over a
medium fire, turning often, until
the kernels turn golden brown,
about 5 minutes. Do not let the
corn burn. Remove the corn
from the grill and serve. Grilled
corn is very messy and very hot,
so try to find some of those cute
little yellow corn holders.

Serves 6

Urban Eating

Grilled Lamb Pita Pocket Sandwiches with Yogurt and Mint

Middle Eastern stores that sell falafel and pita sandwiches are found in just about every New York neighborhood. Grilled cubes of lamb are paired with lettuce and a tangy yogurt sauce for this hearty sandwich.

I	**cup plain yogurt**
3	**tablespoons vegetable oil**
2	**tablespoons lemon juice**
I	**tablespoon minced garlic**
¼	**cup minced fresh mint leaves**
2	**pounds boneless lamb, cut into I ½-inch cubes**
	Salt and ground black pepper
6	**pita breads, warmed**
3	**cups shredded iceberg lettuce**

▶ Combine the yogurt, oil, lemon juice, garlic, and mint in a large bowl. Remove half of mixture, cover, and refrigerate until serving time. Add the lamb to the remaining yogurt mixture and toss well to coat. Cover and refrigerate for at least 1 hour or overnight.

▶ Light the grill. Thread the lamb onto skewers and sprinkle generously with salt and pepper to taste. Scrape the hot grill surface clean. Grill shish kabobs, turning once, until the lamb is cooked the way you like it, about 8 minutes for medium-rare.

▶ Remove the lamb from the skewers and divide among the pita pockets along with the shredded lettuce and the reserved yogurt sauce.

Serves 6

Urban Eating

Manhattan Clam Chowder

Yes, New Yorkers really do spoon up this tomato-based clam broth. The bacon is a must.

4	**slices bacon**
I	**large onion, minced**
I	**rib celery, minced**
I	**28-ounce can whole tomatoes packed in juice**
2	**medium baking potatoes, peeled and cut into ½-inch cubes**
2	**cups water**
½	**cup white wine**
I	**teaspoon dried tarragon**
24	**littleneck clams, shucked and chopped with juices strained and reserved**
¼	**cup minced fresh parsley leaves**
	Salt and ground black pepper

▶ Fry the bacon in a large soup pot or kettle until crisp. Lift the bacon to a plate lined with paper towels. Crumble the bacon when cool and set it aside.

▶ Meanwhile, add the onion and celery to the bacon drippings in the pot. Cook over medium heat until the vegetables are quite soft, about 8 minutes. Coarsely chop the tomatoes and add them to the pot along with their packing liquid. Add the potatoes, water, wine, and tarragon to the pot. Simmer gently until the potatoes are almost tender, about 15 minutes. Add the shucked clams and their strained juices to the pot along with the parsley and crumbled bacon. Simmer just until the clams are cooked through, no more than 5 minutes. Add salt (the soup might not need much) and pepper to taste. Ladle into bowls or mugs and serve hot.

Serves 4 to 6

Joey on Women

"Yes, now is when you swoop. You gotta make sure that when Paolo walks outta here, the first guy Rachel sees is you. She's gotta know that you're everything he's not. You're, like, the Anti-Paolo."

"You don't kiss your friend's mom. Sisters are okay, maybe a hot lookin' aunt, but not a mom, never a mom!"

"I don't know. I loved high school. You know, it was just, like, four years of parties and dating and sex. . . ."

"I met this really hot, single mom at the store. What's an elf to do?"

"Why do you have to break up with her? Be a man. Just stop calling."

"When I'm with a woman, I need to know that I'm going out with more people than she is."

Chandler:
Forget about her!

Joey:
He's right, man. Please. Move on. Go to China. Eat Chinese food.

Chandler:
Of course, there they just call it "food."

Little Italy's Best Linguine with Red Clam Sauce

New Yorkers are not the only ones who love Italian food. This dish is a classic from the city to the country.

3	pounds littleneck clams
1	bay leaf
3	tablespoons olive oil
3	medium cloves garlic, minced
1	28-ounce can crushed tomatoes
1	teaspoon minced fresh oregano leaves or ½ teaspoon dried
	Salt and ground black pepper
1	pound linguine

▶ Bring plenty of water to a boil in a large pot for cooking the pasta. Meanwhile, thoroughly wash and scrub the clams to remove as much sand as possible. Pour ¼ cup cold water into a large pot with a tight lid. Add the bay leaf and clams and bring to a boil over high heat. Steam the clams until most have opened, about 5 minutes. Lift the clams from the pot, leaving behind the juices and discarding any clams that have not opened. Strain the liquid through a sieve lined with a paper towel and reserve; discard the bay leaf. When cool enough to handle, shuck the clams, cut them into bite-sized pieces if necessary, and set them aside separately.

▶ Heat the oil in large saucepan. Add the garlic and sauté over medium heat until golden, about 1 minute. Add the tomatoes and simmer until the sauce thickens considerably, about 10 minutes.

▶ Add ⅓ cup strained clam juice and the oregano to the tomato sauce. (Discard the remaining clam juice.) Simmer until the flavors are blended and the sauce thickens again, 5 to 7 minutes. Add salt and pepper to taste. Remove the pan from the heat and stir in the clams.

▶ While the sauce is simmering, cook and drain the pasta. Toss the hot pasta with the clam sauce. Mix well and transfer portions to pasta bowls. Serve immediately.

Serves 4

TAKEOUT

Intended to be eaten off the premises; selling or intended for the sale of food products to be consumed off the premises.

Pan-Fried Dumplings with Mushrooms and Scallions

Urban dwellers love Chinese food. Maybe it's because Chinese restaurants deliver. Even if you don't feel like takeout—or live in a big city—you can still enjoy Chinese food. These ruffled potstickers are first browned in hot oil to crisp their bottoms. Hot water is then added to the skillet, which is covered to create a moist environment that allows the potstickers to steam.

6	tablespoons vegetable oil
2	medium cloves garlic, minced
1	pound mushrooms, diced small

- **1** **tablespoon soy sauce, plus more for dipping**
- **1** **tablespoon dark sesame oil**
- **3** **medium scallions, white and light green parts minced**
- **1** **tablespoon sesame seeds, toasted**
     Salt and ground black pepper
- **32** **round dumpling wrappers, each about 3 ½ inches in diameter**
- **1** **cup water**

▶ Heat 2 tablespoons oil in a large skillet. Add the garlic and sauté over medium heat until golden, about 2 minutes. Add the mushrooms and sauté, stirring occasionally, until the liquid they throw off has mostly evaporated, about 7 minutes. Stir in the soy sauce, sesame oil, scallions, and sesame seeds and season generously with salt and pepper to taste. Transfer the filling to a bowl and cool to room temperature.

▶ Working with a single wrapper at a time, place 2 teaspoons filling in the center of the wrapper. Moisten the edges with water and fold the wrapper in half over the filling. Use your index finger and thumb to pinch the edges together. Lightly press the filling on the work surface to form a flat base. Gather the pinched edges together to form ruffles on top.

▶ Bring 1 cup water to a boil in a small pan. Meanwhile, divide the remaining 4 tablespoons oil

between two 10-inch skillets. When the oil is hot but not yet smoking, add half the dumplings to each pan, flat sides down. Fry until the bottoms of the dumplings are browned, about 2 minutes.

▶ Pour ½ cup simmering water around the edges of each pan. Cover and cook until the water is absorbed, about 3 minutes. Uncover and continue cooking until the bottoms of the dumplings have become crisp again, another minute or so. Transfer dumplings to a warm platter and serve immediately with soy sauce and chopsticks.

Makes about 32 dumplings, enough for 6 to 8

Ross:
Well I think it's perfect. You know, it's just going to be the two of us. She spent all day taking care of my monkey.

Chandler:
I can't remember the last time I got a girl to take care of my monkey.

Ross:
Anyway, I figured after work, I'd pick up a bottle of wine, go over there, and try to . . . woo her.

Chandler:
Hey, you know what you should do? Take her back to the 1890s when that phrase was last used.

Pizza Guy:
You're not "G. Stephanopoulos"? Oh man, oh man. My dad's gonna kill me.

Monica:
Wait. Did you say "G. Stephanopoulos"?

Pizza Guy:
Yeah. This one goes across the street. I must have given him yours. Bonehead, bonehead.

Monica:
Was he a small, Mediterranean guy with curiously intelligent good looks?

Pizza Guy:
That sounds right.

Monica:
Was he wearing a stunning blue suit?

Phoebe:
Yeah, and a power tie?

Pizza Guy:
Nope. Pretty much just a towel.

Monica and Phoebe:
Oh my god. Wow.

Pizza Guy:
So you want me to take this back?

Monica:
Are you nuts? We've got George Stephanopoulos's pizza!

Rachel:
Who's George Snuffelupagus?

Political Pizza

When the wrong pizza gets delivered to the apartment, the girls are upset—at first. They wanted fat-free crust with extra cheese. What they got, however, was a pie with mushrooms, green peppers, and onions. When they realize this delicious pizza was ordered by the cute Clinton advisor, they decide to make do.

½	**Perfect Pizza Dough (page 82)**
2	**tablespoons olive oil**
I	**small onion, sliced thin**
I	**cup thinly sliced mushrooms**
½	**small green bell pepper, cored, seeded, and diced**
	Salt and ground black pepper
I½	**cups favorite tomato sauce, warmed**
¼	**cup grated Parmesan cheese**
¼	**pound mozzarella cheese, shredded**

▶ Prepare the dough and set it aside to rise.

▶ Heat the oil in a large skillet. Add the onions and cook until soft, about 5 minutes. Add the mushrooms and cook until they give off their juices, about 5 minutes. Add the green peppers and salt and pepper to taste and continue cooking until the peppers soften, about 3 minutes. Stir the vegetables into the tomato sauce and adjust the seasonings.

▶ Place the pizza stone (if using) in the oven and preheat to 500° for 30 minutes. Sprinkle a pizza peel or large rimless baking sheet with cornmeal and roll the dough out into a 12-inch circle. Spread the tomato sauce and vegetables over the dough, leaving a ½-inch border around the edge. Sprinkle with Parmesan and then mozzarella cheese.

▶ If using a stone, slide the pizza from the peel or baking sheet onto the preheated stone. Otherwise, place the baking sheet in the oven. Bake until the cheese starts to brown, 12 to 15 minutes. Remove the pizza from the oven and cut it into wedges. Serve immediately.

Makes one 12-inch pizza, enough for 2 (in case George drops by)

Bagels with Homemade Scallion Cream Cheese

There are those among us who think bagels are New York's greatest gift to the culinary world. When bagels are spread with scallion cream cheese, even doubters will see the light.

½	**pound cream cheese, at room temperature**
¼	**cup sour cream**
¼	**cup minced scallions**
	Salt
6	**large bagels, split**

▶ Stir the cream cheese and sour cream together with a large spatula. Stir in the scallions and add salt to taste. Chill the cream cheese spread and slather liberally on bagels. This spread can also be used as a dip with vegetables or served with crackers.

Serves 6

The ABCs of Pizza

Flat bread topped with sauce is nothing new, possibly dating back to the times of earliest man. But it wasn't until GIs returned home from WW II with their newly acquired tastes for Italian cuisine that pizza became a true American favorite.

Before you start showing off and tossing your dough up in the air, be advised that good pizza calls for good crust. You can mix and knead it either by hand or with a mixer. Make plenty; you can freeze what you don't use. Find a recipe for basic dough that you are comfortable with. Once you have made the dough several times, you can experiment. Adding a little whole-wheat flour, rye flour, or cornmeal will add distinct flavors and textures.

When shaping the dough, flour your hands and work in a circular motion. Flatten it out to a disk about six to eight inches around. Even it out and flip it over. (Show off here if you must!) Stretch the dough carefully until it is about twelve inches in diameter, and pat the edges before transferring it to a pan that has been oiled.

Toppings are limited only by your imagination. Most, such as cured meats or fresh seafood, can be placed uncooked on the dough. But vegetables and some meats, such as sausage, will probably need to be precooked. Vegetables can be grilled or sautéed.

The tastiest crust comes from being baked as close as possible to the oven floor. You can use just about any kind of flat pan, although many people swear by pizza stones or baking tiles.

Monica:
Uh, Pheebs. Remember how we talked about saying things quietly to yourself first?

Phoebe:
Yes. But, there isn't always time.

Pesto Pizza

Pesto on pizza? What will those wacky New Yorkers think of next! Actually, they stole the idea from Italy, but this version is now a classic in chic pizzerias. Because this pie is baked without any toppings, it is necessary to prick the dough all over to prevent large bubbles from forming. The pesto is spread over the crust as soon as it comes out of the oven to make a light pizza that can be served as an appetizer or alongside a bowl of soup. A favorite pesto recipe, either prepared or homemade, may be substituted, if desired.

½   **Perfect Pizza Dough (page 82)**
1   **cup tightly packed fresh basil leaves**
1   **medium clove garlic, peeled**
2   **tablespoons pine nuts or walnuts**
¼   **cup olive oil**
¼   **cup grated Parmesan cheese**
    Salt and ground black pepper

▶   Prepare the dough and set it aside to rise.

▶   Place the basil, garlic, and nuts in the work bowl of a food processor or in a blender. Process, scraping down the sides as needed, until the ingredients are finely chopped. With the motor running, slowly pour the oil through the feed tube and process until smooth. Scrape the pesto into a small bowl and stir in the cheese, salt, and pepper.

▶   Place the pizza stone (if using) in the oven and preheat to 500° for 30 minutes. Sprinkle a pizza peel or large rimless baking sheet with cornmeal and roll the dough out into a 12-inch circle. Prick the dough all over with a fork.

▶   If using a stone, slide the pizza from the peel or baking sheet onto the preheated stone. Otherwise, place the baking sheet in the oven. Bake until the crust begins to brown in spots, about 10 minutes. Remove the crust from the oven and spread lightly with pesto sauce, leaving a ½-inch border around the edge. Cut into wedges and serve immediately.

Makes one 12-inch pizza, enough for 2

"So, who's up for a big game of Kerplunk?**"**

Tomato and Mozzarella Pizza with Basil

Fresh tomatoes make this pizza a summer classic. In the winter, substitute a cup of your favorite tomato sauce. Just spread the sauce over the dough and top with the cheese mixture.

½	**Perfect Pizza Dough (page 82)**
2	**large ripe tomatoes (about 1 pound)**
¼	**pound mozzarella cheese, shredded**
2	**tablespoons olive oil**
2	**medium cloves garlic, minced**
¼	**cup chopped fresh basil leaves**
	Salt and ground black pepper

▶ Prepare the dough and set it aside to rise.

▶ Core the tomatoes and slice them into very thin circles. Lay the tomatoes on paper towels to absorb excess moisture. Combine the cheese, oil, garlic, basil, and salt and pepper to taste in a bowl and set the mixture aside.

▶ Place the pizza stone (if using) in the oven and preheat to 500° for 30 minutes. Sprinkle a pizza peel or large rimless baking sheet with cornmeal and roll the dough out into a 12-inch circle. Line the dough with concentric circles of slightly overlapping tomato slices, leaving a ½-inch border around the edge. Evenly distribute the cheese mixture over the tomatoes.

▶ If using a stone, slide topped pizza from the peel or baking sheet onto the preheated stone. Otherwise, place the baking sheet in the oven. Bake until the cheese starts to brown, 12 to 15 minutes. Remove the pizza from the oven and cut into wedges. Serve immediately.

Makes one 12-inch pizza, enough for 2

"Ugly Naked Guy's laying kitchen tile."

Luisa:
Luisa Gianetti. Lincoln High. I sat behind you guys in homeroom.

Rachel:
Oh, Luisa! Oh my god! Monica! It's Luisa!

Monica:
Oh, sure! Luisa . . . from homeroom!

Luisa:
You have no idea who I am, do you?

Monica and Rachel:
No. Not at all. No.

Luisa:
Well, maybe that's because you spent four years ignoring me. Would it have been so hard to say, "Mornin' Luisa" or "Nice overalls"?

Monica:
Oh, I'm so sorry.

Luisa:
It wasn't so much with you. You were fat. You had your own problems. But you, what a bitch.

Rachel:
Chandler, I've got to tell you, I love your mom's books. I love her books! I cannot get on a plane without one. This is so cool.

Chandler:
Yeah, well, it's not so cool when you're eleven and all your friends are passing around page seventy-nine of Mistress Bitch.

Nora's Kung Pao Chicken

Chandler's famous mom (as played by the way-too-sexy Morgan Fairchild) has a special fondness for this spicy dish. When the gang gathers to watch Nora on television, Chandler cringes as she tells Jay Leno, "All right, this is kind of embarrassing, but occasionally after I've been . . . intimate with a man . . . I get this craving for kung pao chicken." "That's too much information," screams Chandler. You can eat this tasty dish anytime, just don't talk about it on national television.

1¼ **pounds skinless, boneless chicken breast, cut into ¾-inch pieces**

3 **tablespoons soy sauce**

1 **tablespoon dark sesame oil**

1 **tablespoon cider vinegar**

2 **teaspoons dry sherry**

1 **tablespoon cornstarch**

3 **tablespoons vegetable oil**

2 **large cloves garlic, minced**

3 **medium scallions, white and light green parts minced**

1 **tablespoon minced fresh ginger root**

6 to 12 **small dried red chilies**

⅔ **cup unsalted dry-roasted peanuts**

▶ Combine the chicken and 1 tablespoon soy sauce in a small bowl and set it aside to marinate for at least 15 minutes.

▶ Combine the remaining 2 tablespoons soy sauce, sesame oil, vinegar, sherry, and cornstarch in a small bowl. Mix until the sauce is smooth and set it aside.

▶ Heat 2 tablespoons vegetable oil in a wok until hot but not yet smoking. Add the chicken and stir-fry until cooked through, 2 to 3 minutes. Use a slotted spoon to transfer the chicken to a bowl and set it aside.

▶ Heat the remaining tablespoon vegetable oil in the wok for several seconds. Add the garlic, scallions, ginger, and as many dried chilies as you like. Stir-fry until the ingredients are fragrant and the chilies begin to darken, about 30 seconds.

▶ Add the chicken, reserved sauce, and peanuts. Stir-fry until the sauce thickens and the chicken is heated through, another minute or so. Serve with steamed white rice, a steamed vegetable, and plenty of water to put out those mouths on fire.

Serves 4

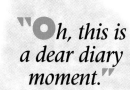

"O*h, this is a dear diary moment.***"**

Vegetarian Delights

Cook and eat—
without the
meat

Phoebe:
She already fluffed that pillow. Monica, you know, you already fluffed that. It's fine.

Monica:
I'm sorry, you guys. I just don't want to give them any more ammunition than they already have.

Chandler:
Yes, and we all know how cruel a parent can be about the flatness of a child's pillow.

Mrs. Geller's Simple Spaghetti

Judy Geller is not the world's most easygoing mother. When she's around, Monica gets even more uptight than usual. (Is that possible?) Nothing Monica does is ever good enough. "Ross, you want to give me a hand with the spaghetti, please?" asks Monica. "Oh, we're having spaghetti. That's . . . easy," responds Mrs. Geller. She's right, of course; mothers usually are. This quick dish with tomatoes and fresh basil is a snap. But did she have to say so?

1	28-ounce can whole tomatoes, drained and chopped
½	cup fresh basil leaves, cut into thin strips
¼	cup olive oil
4	medium cloves garlic, minced
1	teaspoon salt
	Ground black pepper
1	pound spaghetti

▶ Get some water going to cook the pasta. This sauce is so quick (and easy) it will be done by the time you bring the water to a boil and then cook the pasta.

▶ Place the tomatoes, basil, oil, garlic, and salt in a medium saucepan set over medium heat. Simmer, stirring occasionally, until the liquid in the pan thickens and the tomatoes form a rough sauce, about 10 minutes. Add pepper to taste.

▶ While the sauce is simmering, cook and drain the spaghetti. Toss the hot pasta with the tomato sauce. Mix well and transfer portions to warm pasta bowls.

Serves 4

Mr. Geller's Pasta with Sun-Dried Tomatoes

Ross and Monica's father has a sharp business sense, but he missed the boat on sun-dried tomatoes. "I'll tell you one thing," says Jack (as played by Elliott Gould), "I wouldn't mind having a piece of this sun-dried tomato business. Five years ago, if somebody had said to me, 'Here's a tomato that looks like a prune,' I'd have said, 'Get out of my office.'" Who could have known?

20	sun-dried tomatoes packed in olive oil, drained and cut into thin strips
¼	cup shredded fresh basil leaves
2	medium cloves garlic, minced
½	teaspoon salt
½	teaspoon hot red pepper flakes
⅓	cup extra-virgin olive oil
1	pound fusilli

▶ Stir together the sun-dried tomatoes, basil, garlic, salt, hot red pepper flakes, and oil in a large bowl. Set the mixture aside to marinate while you prepare the pasta.

▶ Bring salted water to a boil for cooking the pasta. Add the fusilli and stir occasionally. Cook until the pasta is al dente. Drain the fusilli, making sure to leave a little cooking water clinging to the noodles. Toss the hot pasta with the sun-dried tomato sauce. Mix well and transfer portions to pasta bowls. Serve immediately.

Serves 4

Broccoli Stir-Fry with Lemon-Garlic Sauce

While everyone else is devouring kung pao chicken and egg rolls, Phoebe-esque eaters can enjoy this vegetarian stir-fry along with steamed brown rice. It's just as good with white rice.

5	cups bite-sized broccoli florets
1	large lemon
2	tablespoons soy sauce
2	teaspoons sugar
2	teaspoons cornstarch
2	tablespoons vegetable oil
2	tablespoons minced garlic
1	teaspoon minced fresh ginger root
2	tablespoons sliced scallions

▶ Bring several quarts of water to a boil in a medium pan. Add the broccoli and cook until almost tender, about 2 minutes. Drain the broccoli and set it aside.

▶ Grate the yellow peel from the lemon. (There should be about 1 teaspoon zest.) Halve the lemon and squeeze out juice. (There should be about 3 tablespoons juice.) Combine the lemon zest, lemon juice, soy sauce, and sugar in a small bowl. Mix well. Stir the cornstarch into the sauce until dissolved. Set the sauce aside.

▶ Heat the oil in a large wok or skillet. When the oil is hot but not yet smoking, add the garlic, ginger, and scallions. Stir-fry until the garlic and ginger are fragrant, about 30 seconds. Add the blanched broccoli and the sauce and stir-fry until the

broccoli is heated through and the sauce thickens, 1 to 2 minutes. Remove the wok from heat and serve the stir-fry with steamed rice.

Serves 2 as a main course or 4 as a side dish

Shredded Zucchini with Garlic and Herbs

This simple shredding and drying technique is the best choice when you are pressed for time and want to cook zucchini quickly.

4	medium zucchini (about 1 ⅓ pounds)
3	tablespoons olive oil
2	medium cloves garlic, minced
2	tablespoons minced fresh parsley leaves
	Salt and ground black pepper

▶ Wash and trim ridged ends from the zucchini. Shred the zucchini using the large holes on a box grater or the shredding disk on a food processor. Wrap the shredded zucchini in several layers of paper towels or in a kitchen towel and squeeze gently. Continue squeezing, using new towels if necessary, until the zucchini is fairly dry.

▶ Heat the oil in a large skillet set over medium-high heat. Add the zucchini and garlic and cook, stirring occasionally, until the zucchini is tender, about 7 minutes. Stir in the parsley and salt and pepper to taste.

Serves 4

Chandler:
Oh, I think this is the episode of Three's Company *where there's some kind of misunderstanding.*

Phoebe:
Oh, then I've already seen this one.

Monica:
Aunt Syl. Stop yelling. All I'm saying is if you would've told me vegetarian lasagnas, I would have made vegetarian lasagnas . . . Well, the meat's only every third layer. Maybe you can scrape. Aunt Syl. . . . I did this as a favor. I'm not a caterer. What do you want me to do with a dozen lasagnas? Nice talk, Aunt Syl. You kiss Uncle Freddie with that mouth?

Aunt Syl's Vegetarian Lasagna

This lasagna, chock full of mush-rooms, onions, and peppers should make even finicky Aunt Syl happy.

¼	**cup olive oil**
2	**large onions, sliced thin**
4	**medium cloves garlic, minced**
1	**pound fresh white mushrooms, sliced thin**
2	**large yellow bell peppers, cut into ½-inch dice**
1	**28-ounce can crushed tomatoes**
¼	**cup minced fresh parsley leaves**
1	**teaspoon salt**
½	**teaspoon ground black pepper**
18	**dried lasagna noodles**
1	**pound mozzarella cheese, shredded**

▶ Heat the oil in a large saucepan. Add the onions and cook over medium heat until very soft, about 10 minutes. Stir in the garlic and mushrooms and cook until the mushrooms start to throw off their liquid, about 5 minutes. Stir in the bell peppers and cook for 3 more minutes. Add the tomatoes, parsley, salt, and pepper to the pan and simmer until the sauce thickens, about 10 minutes. Keep the sauce warm.

▶ Cook the lasagna noodles in salted boiling water until almost al dente. Drain, refresh in a bowl of cold water, and drain again. Lay the noodles out on kitchen towels to soak up excess moisture.

▶ Preheat the oven to 400°. Grease a 13 x 9-inch baking dish. Smear several tablespoons of tomato sauce (without large chunks of vegetables) across the bottom of the pan. Line the pan with a layer of pasta, making sure that the noodles touch but do not overlap. Spread 1 cup tomato sauce mixture evenly over the pasta. Sprinkle evenly with ⅔ cup mozzarella. Repeat layering of the pasta, tomato sauce, and cheese 5 more times.

▶ Bake until the cheese on top turns golden brown in spots and the sauce is bubbling, 20 to 25 minutes. Remove the pan from the oven, let the lasagna settle for 5 minutes, and cut it into squares.

Serves 8

Potato Casserole with Spinach, Mushrooms, and Gruyère

This one-dish meal is just the thing for vegetarians in search of hearty fare. Lots of flavor, not too much work, and great with a glass of wine.

6	**large baking potatoes (about 3 pounds)**
6	**tablespoons olive oil**
4	**medium cloves garlic, minced**
1½	**teaspoons salt**
¾	**teaspoon ground black pepper**
1	**medium onion, chopped**
¾	**pound fresh white mushrooms, sliced thin**
1½	**pounds spinach, stemmed and washed**
1½	**cups ricotta cheese**
½	**pound Gruyère cheese, shredded**

▶ Preheat the oven to 400°. Grease 2 large baking sheets and set them aside.

▶ Scrub the potatoes under cold running water but do not peel them. Cut the potatoes lengthwise into ¼-inch-thick slices. Place the slices in a large bowl. Combine 4 tablespoons oil with the garlic, 1 teaspoon salt, and ½ teaspoon pepper in a small bowl. Pour the mixture over the potatoes and toss gently. (With your hands is the easiest, if messiest, way to do this.) Lay the potato slices out on the prepared pans, making sure they do not overlap. Cover the pans tightly with aluminum foil and bake for 30 minutes. Remove the pans from the oven, uncover, and cool. Do not turn off the oven.

▶ While the potatoes are baking, heat the remaining 2 tablespoons oil in a large pot. Add the onion and cook over medium heat until soft, about 5 minutes. Add the mushrooms and cook until they throw off their juices, about 5 minutes more. Stir in the spinach and the remaining ½ teaspoon salt and ¼ teaspoon pepper. Cover and cook until the spinach wilts, about 4 minutes. Uncover and cook off any liquid in the pot. Remove the pot from the heat and stir in the ricotta.

▶ Grease a 13 x 9-inch baking pan. Line the bottom of the pan with ⅓ of the potatoes. Spoon half of the spinach mixture over the potatoes and then sprinkle with ⅓ of the Gruyère. Make another layer of potatoes and cover with remaining spinach mixture and another third of the cheese. Cover with the remaining potatoes and sprinkle with the remaining cheese.

▶ Bake until the casserole turns golden brown on top, about 25 minutes. Remove the pan from the oven and let settle for 5 minutes before cutting up slices.

Serves 6 to 8

"Hello? Kettle?
*This is Monica.
You're black."*

Monica:
Okay. Okay. I got one. Remember the vegetarian pâté I made that you liked so much?

Phoebe:
Uh-huh.

Monica.
Well, unless goose is a vegetable. . . .

Lisa Kudrow / PHOEBE

Lisa Kudrow, who has a degree in biology from Vassar College, got her big break as inept waitress Ursula on the hit series *Mad About You*, a role she continues today. Initially planning to attend medical school and then work with her researcher father, Kudrow also had a recurring role on *Bob*, starred in *Murder in High Places*, and guest starred on *Coach, Flying Blind, Lifestories, Life Goes On, Newhart, Cheers, Room for Two,* and *On the Television*. Her feature film credits include *Heat of Passion, Dance with Death, The Unborn,* and *Impulse*. Kudrow's stage work includes serving as both a regular company member and teacher for the Groundlings, an improvisational theater group in Los Angeles, and starring roles in *Ladies Room, Maps for Drowners,* and *Girls Club*. Kudrow, included in *Esquire* magazine's list of "Women Who Are Probably Not as Wholesome as They Seem" in 1995, is known to play a mean game of pool. (And just for the record, she eats meat.)

Spiced Moroccan Carrots

Cinnamon and cumin make everyday carrots something special. Serve as a side dish, as a room temperature salad, or as a main course with some couscous.

1½	pounds carrots, peeled
¼	cup olive oil
4	teaspoons lime juice
½	teaspoon ground cumin
½	teaspoon ground cinnamon
1	teaspoon salt
3	tablespoons minced fresh parsley leaves

▶ Bring several quarts of water to a boil in a large pot. Add the whole carrots and simmer until they are tender but not soft, about 12 minutes. Drain the carrots and cool slightly.

▶ While the carrots are cooling, whisk the oil, lime juice, spices, and salt together in a medium serving bowl. Cut the carrots into ¼-inch pieces and add them to the bowl with the dressing. Stir in the parsley. Eat warm or cool to room temperature.

Serves 6 as a side dish

Joey's Best Pasta Sauce

Joey doesn't cook very often, but he does know how to make a good tomato sauce. He's Italian, isn't he? This spicy sauce with olives can be made with pantry items, making it perfect for the cook who never has anything fresh in the fridge.

¼   **cup olive oil**

4   **medium cloves garlic, minced**

½   **teaspoon hot red pepper flakes or to taste**

I   **28-ounce can whole tomatoes, drained and chopped**

20 **large olives (either black or green), pitted and chopped**

    Salt

I   **pound spaghetti**

▶   Get some water going to cook the pasta. This sauce will be done by the time the water comes to a boil and you cook the spaghetti.

▶   Heat the oil in a large skillet. Add the garlic and hot pepper flakes and sauté over medium heat until the garlic is golden, about 2 minutes. Add the tomatoes and olives to the pan. Simmer, occasionally using a spoon to break apart the tomatoes, until the sauce thickens, about 15 minutes. Add salt to taste. (Olives are usually quite salty, so the sauce might require very little.)

▶   While preparing the sauce, cook and drain the pasta. Toss the hot pasta with the tomato sauce. Mix well and transfer portions to pasta bowls.

Serves 4

Italian Green Salad with Pine Nuts and Yellow Raisins

An assortment of tender baby greens is tossed with toasted pine nuts and yellow sultana raisins for this simple Italian salad. A lemony dressing adds a bright acidic component that contrasts nicely with the sweetness of the raisins and the richness of the nuts. Any tender young lettuces are appropriate in this salad, preferably a mixture of some of the following: red leaf lettuce, escarole, watercress, young arugula, frisée, escarole, mizuna, and tatsoi. Create your own combination or use the prewashed "gourmet" salad mix sold in many markets.

3   **tablespoons olive oil**

2   **tablespoons lemon juice**

    Salt and ground black pepper

8   **cups washed and dried tender lettuces and baby greens (see note above)**

2   **tablespoons pine nuts, toasted**

2   **tablespoons yellow raisins**

▶   Whisk together the oil, lemon juice, and salt and pepper to taste in a large salad bowl. Add the washed and dried greens, pine nuts, and raisins to the bowl and toss until the lettuces are evenly coated with the dressing. Divide the salad among 4 plates and serve immediately.

Serves 4

Phoebe on Life

"I'm sorry I'm late. I couldn't find my bearings."

"I mean, you're like . . . you're like all chaotic and twirly. And not in the good way."

"Go to your happy place. La la la la la."

"Ooo. I just pulled out four eyelashes. That can't be good."

"Oh, I believe it. I think the baby can totally hear everything. Look, I'll show you. This is going to sound a little weird, but . . . You put your head inside the turkey, and we'll talk, and you'll hear everything we say."

"Okay. Okay. If I were omnipotent for a day, I'd want . . . world peace . . . no more hunger . . . good things for the rain forest . . . and bigger boobs."

"And on my way over here, I stepped in gum. What is up with the universe?"

Chandler:
*All right. Tell you what.
When we're forty, if
neither of us are married,
what do you say you and
I get together.*

Monica:
*Why won't I be married
when I'm forty?*

Chandler:
*Oh no, no. No. I just
meant hypothetically.*

Monica:
*Okay. Hypothetically,
why won't I be married
when I'm forty?*

Chandler:
*It doesn't matter. I just
don't want to be one of
those guys that's in his
office 'til eleven o'clock at
night, worrying about the
WEENUS.*

Grilled Zucchini Salad with Tomatoes and Balsamic Vinaigrette

The zucchini is grilled, cooled briefly, and then tossed with fresh tomatoes and a balsamic vinaigrette for a light meat-free meal. Your carnivorous friends will also like this room temperature salad as a side with grilled steak.

6	medium zucchini (about 2 pounds)
¼	cup olive oil
	Salt and ground black pepper
2	tablespoons balsamic vinegar
2	large ripe tomatoes (about ¾ pound)
¼	cup fresh basil leaves, minced

► Light the grill. Wash and trim ends from the zucchini. Slice the trimmed zucchini lengthwise into ½-inch-thick strips. Lay the zucchini on a large baking sheet and brush both sides with 2 tablespoons oil. Sprinkle generously with salt and pepper.

► Scrape the hot grill surface clean. Grill the zucchini, turning once, until dark grill marks are visible on both sides, about 5 minutes per side. Remove the zucchini from the grill and cool briefly.

► Whisk the remaining 2 tablespoons oil with the balsamic vinegar, 1 teaspoon salt, and ¼ teaspoon pepper. Core and cut the tomatoes into thin wedges. Toss the tomatoes and basil with the dressing in a large bowl.

► Cut the grilled zucchini into 1-inch pieces. Add the zucchini to the bowl with the tomatoes and toss gently. Adjust the seasonings. Serve at once or cover and set aside at room temperature for up to 3 hours.

Serves 4

Green Beans with Pesto

A smooth purée of basil, walnuts, and garlic dresses up plain old green beans. You can serve the beans hot as a side dish or chill them and eat as a cold salad.

1	cup loosely packed fresh basil leaves
2	tablespoons walnuts
1	medium clove garlic, peeled
¼	cup olive oil
½	teaspoon salt
¼	teaspoon ground black pepper
1	pound green beans, ends trimmed

► Place the basil, walnuts, and garlic in the work bowl of a food processor or in a blender. Process, scraping down the sides as needed, until the ingredients are finely chopped. With the motor running, slowly pour the oil through the feed tube and process until smooth. Scrape the pesto into a large bowl. Stir in the salt and pepper and set aside briefly while cooking the beans.

► Bring some water to a boil in a steamer pot. Place the beans in the top part of the steamer and cook until tender, about 6 minutes. Let any water drip from the beans and then place them into the bowl with the pesto. Toss gently and adjust the seasonings.

Serves 4

Vegetarian Caesar Salad

No eggs or anchovies here but lots of garlic, cheese, and lemon. The toasted croutons are a must, so don't even think about leaving them out.

½   **loaf Italian or French bread**

½   **cup olive oil, plus 2 tablespoons**

I   **large clove garlic, peeled**

3   **tablespoons lemon juice**

I   **teaspoon Dijon mustard**

½   **teaspoon Worcestershire sauce**
     Salt and ground black pepper

I   **large head romaine lettuce, washed and torn into bite-sized pieces**

½   **cup grated Parmesan cheese**

▶ Cut the bread into 1-inch croutons. Heat 2 tablespoons oil in a large nonstick skillet. Add the croutons and cook, turning once, until golden, 5 minutes. Transfer the croutons to a plate lined with paper towels. Set the croutons aside.

▶ Place the garlic in the work bowl of a food processor or in a blender. Process, scraping down the sides as needed, until finely chopped. Add the lemon juice, mustard, and Worcestershire sauce and process until smooth. With the motor running, slowly pour the remaining ½ cup oil through the feed tube and process until the dressing is smooth. Pour the dressing into a small bowl. Add salt and pepper to taste.

▶ Toss the lettuce, dressing, cheese, and croutons together in a large bowl. Mix well. Divide the salad among individual plates.

Serves 2 for lunch or 4 as a first course for dinner

Fusilli with Summer Tomato Sauce and Arugula

A simple fresh tomato sauce with olive oil and garlic is tossed with fusilli and a handful of chopped raw arugula for a quick summer dish. The tomatoes are really just warmed in the hot oil and should not be cooked long. The arugula "cooks" on contact with the hot pasta.

4   **cups stemmed arugula leaves**

3   **medium ripe tomatoes (about I ¼ pounds)**

3   **tablespoons olive oil**

2   **medium cloves garlic, minced**

I   **teaspoon salt**

I   **pound fusilli**

▶ Bring water to a boil in a large pot for cooking the pasta. Wash and dry the arugula. Slice the arugula leaves crosswise into thin strips and set them aside in a bowl large enough to hold the cooked pasta. Core and cut the tomatoes into ½-inch cubes and set them aside separately.

▶ Heat the oil in a large skillet. Add the garlic and sauté over medium heat until lightly colored, about 2 minutes. Add the tomatoes and salt and cook, stirring occasionally, just until the tomatoes are heated through, about 2 minutes.

▶ While preparing the sauce, cook and drain the pasta. Toss the pasta and tomato sauce with the arugula. Mix well until the arugula wilts. Divide portions among pasta bowls and serve immediately.

Serves 4

Ursula:
Want some chicken?

Phoebe:
No. Remember? No food with a face.

Chandler:
Can you see my nipples through this shirt?

Rachel:
No. But don't worry, I'm sure they're still there.

Risotto with Carrots and Peas

This Italian rice dish is a perfect main course for vegetarians. Canned vegetable broth is sold in supermarkets and works well in this recipe. Arborio rice, an Italian variety, is essential here. Look for it in gourmet stores as well as many supermarkets.

6	**cups vegetable broth**
3	**tablespoons olive oil**
1	**medium onion, chopped**
2	**medium cloves garlic, minced**
2	**cups arborio rice**
½	**cup white wine**
4	**medium carrots, peeled and chopped**
2	**cups fresh green peas or frozen peas, thawed**
2	**tablespoons minced fresh parsley leaves**
1	**tablespoon butter**
½	**cup grated Parmesan cheese, plus more for the table**
	Salt and ground black pepper

► Bring the vegetable broth to a boil in a medium saucepan. Keep the broth warm over low heat.

► Meanwhile, heat the oil in a large saucepan. Add the onion and sauté over medium heat until soft, about 5 minutes. Stir in the garlic and continue cooking for another minute. Stir in the rice and cook for 30 seconds or until rice is well coated with the oil. Add the wine and simmer, stirring constantly, until the alcohol aroma fades, about 2 minutes.

► Add the carrots and ½ cup hot broth. Stir constantly until the liquid is absorbed. Continue adding more of the broth in ½-cup increments. When the rice has absorbed most of the broth and is almost al dente, stir in the peas and parsley. Continue cooking and stirring, adding more liquid as necessary, until the rice is creamy and al dente. If you run out of broth, add hot water.

► Remove the rice from the heat and stir in the butter, Parmesan, and salt and pepper to taste. Serve immediately with more grated cheese passed separately at the table.

Serves 4 as a main course or 6 as an elegant appetizer

Brown Rice and Chickpea Salad

Brown rice might be a health food cliché, but it does taste good, especially with chickpeas and the basil-curry dressing in this main-course summer salad.

3   **cups cooked brown rice**

1   **19-ounce can chickpeas, drained and rinsed**

1   **large red bell pepper, cored, seeded, and diced small**

¼   **cup sliced almonds, lightly toasted**

¼   **cup olive oil**

1½   **tablespoons lemon juice**

1½   **tablespoons white vinegar**

½   **teaspoon curry powder**

¾   **teaspoon salt**

3   **tablespoons minced fresh basil leaves**

▶ Prepare the brown rice according to package directions. Fluff 3 cups cooked rice with a fork and cool slightly. Stir in the chickpeas, bell pepper, and toasted almonds.

▶ Whisk the oil, lemon juice, vinegar, curry, and salt together in a small bowl until smooth. Stir in the basil. Drizzle the dressing over the brown rice salad and mix well until the salad is evenly coated with dressing. Serve the salad slightly warm, at room temperature, or chilled over salad greens.

Serves 4

Couscous Salad with Cucumber and Cherry Tomatoes

Couscous is a North African pasta that does not require any cooking. Simply stir the tiny granules into boiling water, cover the pot, and set aside for 5 minutes to allow the couscous to soften and swell. Serve some bread with this room temperature grain-and-vegetable salad to make a complete summer meal.

2¼   **cups water**

1   **10-ounce box couscous**

1½   **teaspoons salt**

1   **medium cucumber**

1   **pint cherry tomatoes, halved**

2   **tablespoons minced fresh mint leaves**

⅓   **cup olive oil**

2   **tablespoons lemon juice**

¼   **teaspoon ground black pepper**

6   **cups washed salad greens**

▶ Bring the water to a boil in a small saucepan. Stir in the couscous and ½ teaspoon salt. Cover the pan and remove it from the heat. Let stand for 5 minutes. Remove the cover and fluff the couscous with a fork. Turn the couscous into a large bowl and cool for at least 20 minutes while you get the rest of the ingredients together.

▶ Peel and halve the cucumber. Use a small spoon to scoop out and discard the seeds from each half of the cucumber. Cut the cucumber into ½-inch pieces. Add the cucumber, tomatoes, and mint to the cooled couscous.

▶ Whisk the oil, lemon juice, remaining teaspoon salt, and pepper together in a small bowl. Drizzle the dressing over the salad and toss gently. Divide salad greens among 4 plates. Spoon some of the couscous over each plate. Serve immediately.

Serves 4

🌿 **CURRY** 🌿
**A mixture of spices that may include:
cardamom, cayenne or other chilies,
cinnamon, clove, coriander, cumin, fennel,
fenugreek, garlic, ginger, and turmeric.
Common in Indian cuisine.**

Monica:
But, you see, it just . . . this night has got to go perfect. And . . . Wendy's more of a professional waitress.

Rachel:
Oh, I see. Yes, and I've sort of been maintaining my amateur status so I can waitress in the Olympics?!

Chandler:
You know, I don't mean to brag, but I waited tables at Innsbruck in '76.

Feisty Black Bean Soup

This classic Mexican soup flavored with peppers and lime meets Phoebe's requirement of "no food with a face." A bottle of well-made beer lends a pleasant, yeasty flavor as well as a touch of sweetness. If you like, omit the beer and increase the water to 2½ cups.

¼	cup vegetable oil
2	medium onions, chopped
4	medium cloves garlic, minced
2	small jalapeño peppers, stemmed and minced
1	tablespoon ground cumin
1	tablespoon chili powder
	Salt
1½	cups beer
1	cup cold water
3	19-ounce cans black beans, drained and rinsed
2	tablespoons fresh lime juice
	Chopped scallions for garnish

▶ Heat the oil in a large soup kettle or stock pot. Add the onions and sauté over medium heat until translucent (or your eyes have stopped tearing), about 5 minutes. Stir in the garlic and jalapeños and cook until the garlic is golden, about 2 minutes.

▶ Add the cumin, chili powder, and a generous amount of salt and stir-cook until the spices are fragrant, about 1 minute. Pour the beer and water into the pot. Bring the mixture to a boil and simmer for 5 minutes. Add the beans and bring the soup back to a boil. Simmer until the soup thickens and the flavors blend, about 10 minutes.

▶ Remove 2 cups of the soup from the pot and purée in a food processor or blender. Return the puréed soup to the pot. Add the lime juice and adjust the seasonings. (Add more spices, salt, or even bottled hot sauce, if you like.)

▶ Ladle the soup into bowls and garnish with chopped scallions. Serve immediately.

Serves 6

Vegging Out

The term *vegetarian* seems to be attributed to a British society of the 1800s. Early vegetarians include Voltaire and Benjamin Franklin. Our contemporary favorite: Phoebe. With more than twelve million Americans now claiming to be vegetarians, we must be warming up to the concept.

Citing reasons from improved health to animal welfare, more and more of us are looking to vegetarianism as a way of life. If you're thinking about forsaking meat, here are a few things to consider.

Becoming a vegetarian might not be as tough as you think. And, of course, there are degrees. Some vegetarians occasionally eat chicken and fish. Others who don't eat any animals or their byproducts at all, are known as *vegans*. More and more restaurants are offering vegetarian dishes, and many of the frozen entrées at your supermarket come sans meat.

In order for you to construct a well-balanced diet without meat, you'll need to retrain your taste buds to crave four main food groups: grains, legumes, nuts, and seeds; vegetables; fruit; and milk and eggs (if you're not going whole hog, so to speak). Through experimentation, you'll find no-meat dishes that you enjoy. Be patient. Some vegetarians suggest starting out by eliminating one meat or dairy product at a time.

Phoebe:
Can you see me operating a drill press?

Joey:
I don't know. What are you wearing?

Spicy Moroccan Lentil Soup

This is as simple as soup gets. Prepare all the ingredients, dump them in a pot, turn on the stove, and simmer for an hour or so. (Spy on the neighbors, take down the Christmas lights—carefully, or whine on the couch while you wait.) Unlike other legumes, dried lentils cook very quickly and do not need to be soaked.

1¼	**cups lentils**
1½	**cups canned whole tomatoes, chopped**
1	**medium onion, chopped**
4	**medium cloves garlic, minced**
4	**medium scallions, white and light green parts sliced thin**
¼	**cup chopped fresh Italian parsley leaves**
¼	**cup chopped fresh cilantro leaves**
1	**tablespoon ground turmeric**
1	**tablespoon ground ginger**
1	**tablespoon paprika**
	Salt and cayenne pepper to taste
5	**cups cold water**
	Parsley or cilantro leaves for garnish

▶ Pick through the lentils and remove any stones or foreign matter. (As strange as it sounds, bags of lentils sometimes contain little pebbles.) Rinse the lentils and place them in a large soup kettle or stock pot. Add the remaining ingredients, except for the garnish, to the pot. Turn the heat to medium and bring the mixture to a boil. Simmer gently until the soup thickens and the flavors blend, about 1 hour.

▶ Remove 1 cup of soup from the pot and purée in a food processor or blender. Return the puréed soup to the pot. Adjust the seasonings.

▶ Ladle the soup into warm bowls and garnish with fresh herbs. Serve immediately.

Serves 6

Roasted New Potatoes, Italian Style

Italians roast new potatoes with garlic and rosemary for a simple side dish that goes with almost everything. These potatoes are especially wonderful with some eggs for a hearty breakfast.

1½	**pounds small new potatoes**
¼	**cup olive oil**
1	**tablespoon minced fresh garlic**
2	**teaspoons minced fresh rosemary leaves or 1 teaspoon dried**
1	**teaspoon salt**
½	**teaspoon ground black pepper**

▶ Preheat the oven to 400°. Scrub the potatoes under cold, running water. Cut the potatoes into ½-inch pieces. Toss the potatoes with 2 tablespoons oil until evenly coated. Spread the potatoes out in a single layer in a large roasting pan. Bake for 30 minutes, turning the potatoes once.

▶ Stir together the remaining 2 tablespoons oil, garlic, rosemary, salt, and pepper. Pour this mixture over the potatoes and toss gently. Continue roasting until the potatoes are golden brown and crisp, 10 to 20 minutes.

Serves 4

Pasta Primavera

With its contrasting flavors and colors, this sauce is the perfect way to celebrate spring. There are several components to this dish that must be prepared separately—blanched green vegetables, sautéed mushrooms, and a garlic, plum tomato, and basil sauce. The vegetables are cooked, added to the mushrooms, and bound with a little cream to form the sauce for the pasta. The tomato mixture is tossed with the drained pasta to give the dish some color and provide extra moisture.

2   cups small broccoli florets

2   cups frozen peas

2   cups thin asparagus, cut into ½-inch pieces

2   tablespoons olive oil

4   medium cloves garlic, minced

½   teaspoon hot red pepper flakes or to taste

¾   pound ripe plum tomatoes, cored and cut into ½-inch cubes

12   large fresh basil leaves, cut into thin strips
    Salt

2   tablespoons unsalted butter

½   pound fresh mushrooms, stems trimmed and thinly sliced

⅓   cup heavy cream

½   cup grated Parmesan cheese, plus more for the table

1   pound linguine

▶ Bring several quarts of water to a boil in a medium saucepan. Add the broccoli, peas, and asparagus and cook until crisp-tender, about 2 minutes. Drain the vegetables and set them aside.

▶ Heat the oil in a medium pan. Add half the garlic and all of the hot pepper flakes and sauté over medium heat until the garlic is golden, about 2 minutes. Add the tomatoes and cook, stirring occasionally, until heated through, about 3 minutes. Stir in the basil and salt to taste. Cover and set aside to keep warm.

▶ Melt the butter in a skillet large enough to hold the mushrooms and the vegetables. Add the remaining garlic and sauté over medium heat until golden, about 2 minutes. Add the sliced mushrooms and cook, stirring often, until they release their juices, about 6 minutes. Season generously with salt.

▶ Drain any liquid that has accumulated at the bottom of the bowl with the blanched vegetables. Add the vegetables to the pan with the mushrooms. Cook, tossing several times, until heated through, about 2 minutes.

▶ Add the cream to pan with the mushrooms and vegetables. Simmer until the sauce thickens a bit, 2 to 3 minutes. Taste for salt and hot pepper and adjust seasonings, if necessary.

▶ While preparing the sauce, cook and drain the pasta. Toss the hot pasta with the vegetable and mushroom mixture, the tomatoes, and ½ cup grated cheese. Mix well and transfer portions to warm pasta bowls. Serve immediately with more grated cheese passed separately, if desired.

Serves 4

Rachel:
What are you playing with?

Ross:
It's my new beeper.

Joey:
What the hell's a paleontologist need a beeper for?

Monica:
Is it for, like, dinosaur emergencies? "Help! Come quick! They're still extinct!"

Phoebe:

Ooo. This is cool. It says that in some parts of the world, people actually eat the placenta.

Chandler:

And we're done with the yogurt.

Grilled Portobello Mushrooms, Red Onions, and Bell Peppers

Portobello mushrooms are particularly "meaty" and stand up well to the intense heat of the grill. Serve with pita breads or brown rice and some plain yogurt. Squeeze the grilled lemon wedges over the brochettes at the table.

¼	**cup olive oil**
2	**tablespoons lemon juice, plus another lemon cut into 8 wedges**
2	**medium cloves garlic, minced**
I	**tablespoon minced fresh mint leaves**
I	**tablespoon minced fresh oregano leaves**
I	**teaspoon salt**
½	**teaspoon ground black pepper**
3	**large portobello mushrooms or I pound white mushrooms**
4	**small red onions, cut into ¾-inch wedges**
2	**medium red bell peppers, cut into I-inch wedges**

▶ Whisk the oil, lemon juice, garlic, herbs, salt, and pepper together in a small bowl. Set the marinade aside.

▶ Remove and discard the stems from the portobello mushrooms. (If using regular white mushrooms, trim a thin slice from each stem.) Wipe dirt from mushrooms with a towel and slice into 1-inch chunks. (Leave small white mushrooms whole.)

▶ Thread mushrooms, onions, and bell peppers alternately on 8 skewers. Thread a lemon wedge on the end of each skewer. Place skewers in a deep baking dish and brush with the marinade. Marinate at room temperature for about 30 minutes.

▶ Light the fire. When hot, scrape the grill surface clean. Place the skewers on the grill and brush with any marinade that is still left in the baking dish. Grill, turning the skewers once or twice, until the vegetables are marked with dark stripes, about 10 minutes. Remove them from the grill and serve immediately.

Serves 4

Sumptuous Desserts

Topping it off
with flair

Joey and Chandler:
You got into San Diego!
You got into San Diego!

Ross:
What?

Joey:
*We were coming back
from our walk and the
phone was ringing and—*

Chandler:
He's in!

Ross:
*Did you hear that,
Marcel?! San Diego!
San Diego!*

Dr. Baldharar:
*You're making a big
mistake here. San Diego's
very well and good. But if
you give him to me, I'll
start him off against a
blind rabbit and give you
twenty percent of the gate.*

Marcel's Splits

Ross's pet monkey might be gone, but he's not forgotten. Make these decadent banana splits in his honor. Roasting the bananas makes them especially sweet, and the Rum-Toffee Sauce gives them a tropical flavor.

Rum-Toffee Sauce

⅔	cup packed light brown sugar
¼	cup heavy cream
5	tablespoons unsalted butter
I	tablespoon rum
½	teaspoon vanilla extract

Splits

4	ripe bananas
	Toppings of your choice
I	pint vanilla ice cream
	Whipped cream (a lot or a little, depending on the kind of day you had)

▶ Preheat the oven to 350°. While the oven is warming up, mix the brown sugar, cream, butter, and rum in a small pan. Bring to a boil and simmer until the sugar dissolves and the sauce thickens a bit, about 2 minutes. Take the pan off the heat and stir in the vanilla extract. Cover the sauce to keep it warm, and try not to eat too much while you roast the bananas.

▶ Place the bananas on a baking sheet and roast in the preheated oven until the skins blacken, about 10 minutes.

While the bananas are in the oven, search your refrigerator and pantry for toppings. Chopped nuts, shredded coconut, fresh berries, and even peanut butter are great on banana splits.

▶ Once the banana skins blacken, remove the bananas from the oven and cool until warm to the touch. If you can't wait (and you won't be able to), put on some oven mitts and use a knife, scissors, or any other sharp instrument at hand to slit the skins opens. Discard the banana skins or save them for a practical joke.

▶ Slice each peeled banana in half lengthwise and place 2 halves in each bowl. Top with ice cream, Rum-Toffee Sauce, whipped cream, and anything else you have uncovered in the fridge or cupboard.

Serves 4

Sumptuous Desserts

Apple Crisp

This all-American classic is remarkably easy to prepare. It's the perfect choice when serving a complicated meal such as Thanksgiving dinner. The crisp can be assembled in a matter of minutes and is foolproof. Serve warm with whipped cream or vanilla ice cream.

8	medium McIntosh apples
¾	cup chopped walnuts
I	cup flour
⅔	cup firmly packed brown sugar
½	teaspoon ground cinnamon
8	tablespoons (I stick) unsalted butter, cut into small pieces
	Vanilla ice cream or whipped cream, optional

► Preheat the oven to 375°. Peel, core, and thinly slice the apples. Arrange the slices in a 13x9-inch ceramic or glass pan that measures about 2 inches deep. The apples should come almost to the top of the pan.

► Combine the nuts, flour, sugar, and cinnamon in a medium bowl. Use your fingers or a fork to work in the butter. The mixture should resemble very coarse crumbs when you are done.

► Sprinkle the topping evenly over the apples. Bake until the filling is bubbling and the topping turns golden brown, about 35 minutes. Serve warm with vanilla ice cream or whipped cream, if desired.

Serves 8

Black-and-White Chocolate Chip Cookies

Phoebe and Ursula might share the same genes—"a twin thing"— but it's hard to imagine two sisters who are more different. These extra-large cookies play off the same dichotomy.

I	cup flour
¼	cup unsweetened cocoa
½	teaspoon baking soda
½	teaspoon salt
8	tablespoons (I stick) unsalted butter, softened
¾	cup sugar
I	large egg
½	teaspoon vanilla extract
I	cup (6 ounces) white chocolate chips
½	cup chopped walnuts

► Preheat the oven to 375°. Stir the flour, cocoa, baking soda, and salt together in a small bowl and set it aside. Cream the butter and sugar with an electric mixer until light and fluffy, about 1 minute. Beat in the egg and vanilla until smooth. Slowly beat in the dry ingredients. Stir in the chocolate chips and nuts.

► For each cookie, drop a little less than ¼ cup batter onto an ungreased large baking sheet. With your hand, slightly flatten each piece of dough. Leave at least 2 inches between each ball. You will need 2 baking sheets to accommodate all the dough.

► Bake until the edges and tops of cookies are set, 15 to 18 minutes. Transfer the cookies to a rack and cool briefly. Eat warm or at room temperature. These cookies will stay nice and chewy for a couple of days.

Makes 12 oversized cookies

Melanie:
I got to tell you, Joey. You are nothing like I thought you would be.

Joey:
How do you mean?

Melanie:
I don't know. I guess I just had you pegged as one of those guys who are always "me, me, me." But you, you're a giver. You're like the most generous man I ever met. I mean, you're practically a woman.

Phoebe:
Okay. We haven't known each other for that long a time. And there are three things you should know about me. One, my friends are the most important thing in my life. Two, I never lie. And three, I make the best oatmeal-raisin cookies in the world.

Rachel:
Okay. Thanks, Pheebs. Why haven't I tasted these before?

Phoebe:
Well, I don't make them a lot. Because I don't think it's fair to the other cookies.

Phoebe's Fabulous Oatmeal-Raisin Cookies

These cookies are so good that Phoebe usually keeps them to herself. Whip up a batch when only the best will do.

12	tablespoons (1½ sticks) unsalted butter, softened
¾	cup firmly packed brown sugar
⅔	cup granulated sugar
1	large egg
1	teaspoon vanilla extract
2	cups old-fashioned rolled oats
1¼	cups flour
¾	teaspoon baking powder
¾	teaspoon baking soda
¼	teaspoon salt
1½	cups raisins

▶ Preheat the oven to 375°. Cream the butter and sugars with an electric mixer until light and fluffy, about 1 minute. Beat in the egg and vanilla until smooth.

▶ Stir together the oats, flour, baking powder, baking soda, and salt in a medium bowl. Stir the dry ingredients into the batter until just combined. Stir in the raisins.

▶ Drop the dough by heaping tablespoons onto 2 large baking sheets (no need to grease them), leaving 2 inches between each ball of dough. Bake until the cookies are golden brown, 12 to 15 minutes. Cool cookies on sheets for several minutes and then transfer them to a rack to cool further.

Makes about 24 large cookies

Peaches Poached in Red Wine with Lemon and Fennel

Poaching peaches in red wine gives them a lovely crimson hue and rich flavor. Serve poached peaches as is with their syrup. Better yet, dollop peaches with a scoop of vanilla ice cream. Choose a young, fruity red wine, like a Beaujolais, for the poaching syrup.

2	cups fruity red wine
1	cup water
½	cup honey
1	lemon
1	teaspoon fennel seeds
2	pounds ripe peaches, peeled, halved, and pitted
	Fresh mint sprigs or very thin slices of lemon for garnish, optional
	Vanilla ice cream, optional but very good

▶ Mix the wine, water, and honey in a large pot. Use a vegetable peeler to remove a long strip of peel from the lemon. (Do not remove any of the white pith.) Add the lemon zest and fennel seeds to the pot. Bring the mixture to a boil and simmer for 10 minutes.

▶ Add the peaches to the poaching liquid. Reduce the heat and cook at the barest simmer until the fruit can be easily pierced with a metal skewer, 5 to 10 minutes depending on its ripeness. Use a slotted spoon to transfer the peaches to a large bowl, leaving behind the lemon peel and as many of the fennel seeds as possible.

► Raise the heat to high and simmer the poaching liquid briskly until reduced to 1 ½ cups, about 10 minutes. Pour the liquid through a fine-mesh strainer and into the bowl with the peaches; discard the fennel seeds and lemon zest. Cool the fruit and poaching syrup to room temperature, cover, and refrigerate for several hours until well chilled. (Peaches can be refrigerated in syrup overnight.)

► Divide peaches among dessert bowls or goblets. Cover with as much poaching syrup as desired. Garnish with sprigs of fresh mint and/or lemon slices and dollop with ice cream, if desired.

Serves 4

Paolo's Strawberries with Balsamic Vinegar

This might sound like an odd combination, but it works and it's oh-so-sophisticated, just like Rachel's Italian ex. The Italians came up with the idea, but this is now the trendy dessert for dieters. When the berries are tossed with sugar and left to stand, the sugar slowly dissolves and forms a rich syrup. A touch of balsamic vinegar balances the sweetness and gives the syrup more body. Even not-so-sweet berries burst with flavor.

2   pints fresh strawberries
3 to 4 tablespoons sugar
l   tablespoon balsamic vinegar

► Hull the strawberries and trim any unripe portions. Slice small berries in half; cut larger berries into 3 or 4 thick slices. In either case, cut from the stem end through the pointed bottom of the berries.

► Place the sliced berries in a large glass or ceramic bowl and toss gently with 3 tablespoons sugar. If the berries are particularly tart, add 1 more tablespoon sugar. Let the berries stand at room temperature, tossing occasionally, to help the sugar to dissolve. After about 30 minutes, the sugar will have formed a thick, red syrup.

► Gently toss the berries with the vinegar. Divide the berries and syrup among 4 bowls or glass goblets and serve immediately.

Serves 4

Ross:
Do you know the word "crap weasel"?

Paolo:
No.

Ross:
Because you are a huge "crap weasel." True story.

Ross on Lost Love

"This was Carol's favorite beer. She always drank it out of the can. I should have known."

"So he's calling from Rome. I could do that. You just got to go to Rome."

"I wanted this to work so much. I mean, I'm still in there. Changing his diapers. Picking his fleas. But he's just phoning it in. It's so hard to accept the fact that something you love so much doesn't love you back, you know?"

"Oh. Uh . . . I just came by to pick up my skull. Well, not mine. . . ."

"Wasn't this supposed to be just a fling? Shouldn't it be . . . flung by now?"

"Okay, I'm gonna play the sperm card one more time."

Blueberry Cobbler

This summer dessert is easy to prepare and incredibly delicious. Vanilla ice cream or whipped cream can be added, but the cobbler itself is quite rich and really needs no embellishment.

3   cups blueberries
⅓   cup orange juice
¾   cup flour
¼   teaspoon baking powder
      Pinch of salt
8   tablespoons (1 stick) unsalted butter, softened
½   cup sugar
1   large egg
½   teaspoon vanilla extract

► Preheat the oven to 375°. Toss the berries and orange juice in an 8-inch-square glass or ceramic baking dish that measures about 2 inches deep. Set the dish aside.

► Whisk the flour, baking powder, and salt together in a small bowl. Set it aside. Cream the butter and sugar with an electric mixer until light and fluffy, about 1 minute. Beat in the egg and vanilla until smooth. Slowly incorporate the dry ingredients using the low setting on the mixer.

► Drop the batter by rounded tablespoons over the berry filling. Cover as much of the surface as possible with small clumps of batter. (Some uncovered spots will remain, but they should be fairly small.)

► Bake until the crust is golden brown and the berry filling is bubbling, 35 to 40 minutes.

Remove the pan from the oven and cool briefly. Serve as is or with whipped cream or vanilla ice cream.

Serves 6

Cranberry-Pear Pie

This easy pie is perfect for the holidays. Serve slices à la mode with vanilla ice cream or with whipped cream, if desired. If using fresh cranberries, rinse and pick through them to remove any that are soft. Frozen cranberries should be used straight from the freezer without thawing.

Pastry
2 ⅓ cups flour
¾   teaspoon salt
1   tablespoon sugar
18   tablespoons (2 ¼ sticks) chilled unsalted butter
5 to 6 tablespoons ice water

Filling
2   medium pears
2 ½ cups fresh or frozen cranberries (about 10 ounces)
⅓   cup orange juice
1   cup sugar
      Milk for brushing on pastry
      Vanilla ice cream or whipped cream, optional only if on a diet

► Place the flour, salt, and sugar in the work bowl of a food processor. Pulse until well blended. Cut the butter into small pieces and add it to the work bowl. Pulse until the mixture resembles coarse crumbs. Turn the mixture in a large bowl.

Work 4 tablespoons water into the dough with a fork or spatula. If the dough seems dry, add more water one tablespoon at a time just until the dough comes together. Divide the dough into two balls, with one slightly larger than the other, and flatten both into 5-inch disks. Wrap disks in plastic and refrigerate while you are making the pie filling.

▶ Peel, core, and halve the pears. Cut the pears into ½-inch cubes and place them in a large bowl. Add 1½ cups cranberries. Place the remaining cranberries, orange juice, and sugar in the work bowl of a food processor. Process until fairly smooth. Scrape the mixture into the bowl with the pears and whole cranberries. Stir until well combined. Set the mixture aside while you roll out the dough.

▶ Adjust rack to lower third position and preheat the oven to 375°. Roll the larger ball into a 12-inch circle and fit the dough into 9-inch pie pan, leaving excess to hang over the rim of the pan. Roll the second ball into an 11-inch circle. Spoon the cranberry-pear mixture and any juices that have accumulated in the bowl into the pie pan. Carefully place the top dough over the filling. Trim top and bottom pieces of dough to within ¼ inch of rim. Press them together and flute as desired. Cut four short slits at right angles in the center of the top crust to allow steam to escape during

baking. Brush top crust with a little milk.

▶ Place the pie pan on a large baking sheet and slide it into the oven. Bake until the crust browns nicely and the juices are bubbling, about 50 minutes. Transfer the pie pan to a rack and cool for at least 1 hour. (The pie can be covered with plastic wrap and set aside at room temperature for up to 6 hours. The pie can be reheated in a warm oven before cutting and serving.)

▶ Cut into wedges and top warm pie with ice cream or whipped cream.

Serves 8

Rachel:
Come on. He's right. Tit for tat.

Chandler:
Well, I am not showing you my tat.

"Are there no conscious men in the city for you two?**"**

Joey:
Let me tell you somethin', there's lots of flavors out there. There's Rocky Road and Cookie Dough and Bing Cherry Vanilla. You can get 'em with jimmies or nuts or whipped cream. This is the best thing that ever happened to you! You got married, you were like what, eight? Welcome back to the world! Grab a spoon!

Ross:
I honestly don't know if I'm hungry or horny.

Chandler:
Then stay out of my freezer.

Ross:
"Grab a spoon." Do you know how long it's been since I grabbed a spoon? Do the words "Billy, don't be a hero" mean anything to you?

Ice Cream Sundaes with Raspberry Sauce

Joey thinks of women in terms of ice cream flavors, among other things. Despite a stirring pep talk, Ross isn't so sure he's ready to dig right in. This raspberry sauce sundae, with nuts and whipped cream, should encourage even the most reluctant dater (or eater).

1	**pint fresh raspberries or 12 ounces frozen berries, thawed**
3 to 4	**tablespoons sugar, depending on the sweetness of the fruit**
2	**tablespoons cold water**
1½	**pints favorite ice cream (Bing Cherry Vanilla sounds good)**
1	**cup whipped cream**
⅓	**cup chopped walnuts**

▶ Place the raspberries, 3 tablespoons sugar, and the water in the work bowl of a food processor or in a blender. Process, scraping down the sides as needed, until smooth. Pour the sauce through a fine-mesh strainer to remove the seeds. (You might need to use a rubber spatula to press the sauce through the mesh.) Taste the sauce and stir in more sugar if desired.

▶ Scoop ice cream into 4 bowls and drizzle each portion with several tablespoons of raspberry sauce. Dollop with whipped cream and sprinkle with nuts.

Serves 4

 S O U F F L É
From the French word meaning "puffed." Made from a sauce base, with whipped egg whites and flavorings. The mixture puffs during cooking because of the egg whites.

Individual Chocolate Soufflés

This cross between a baked pudding and a soufflé is incredibly rich and quite easy to prepare. Baking part of the soufflés in a water bath tames the heat of the oven and ensures a moist texture. This recipe can be cut in half if making dessert for a romantic dinner for two. But then again, they're so good you may each want to eat two.

6	**ounces semisweet or bittersweet chocolate**
8	**tablespoons (1 stick) unsalted butter**
4	**large eggs**
1	**cup flour**
½	**teaspoon baking powder**
¼	**teaspoon salt**
1	**teaspoon vanilla extract**
1	**cup sugar**
	Confectioners' sugar for dusting soufflés

▶ Preheat the oven to 350°. Place a large baking pan in the center of the oven and fill it with about ½ inch of warm water.

▶ Melt the chocolate and butter together in the top of a double boiler or in a microwave set to medium power, stirring occasionally until smooth. Set the mixture aside to cool slightly.

▶ While the chocolate and butter are melting, place the uncracked eggs in a small bowl and cover with warm water. Set aside for 5 minutes. Briefly whisk the flour, baking powder, and salt together in a small bowl. Set the mixture aside.

▶ Crack the eggs into a large bowl and add the vanilla. Beat with an electric mixer until foamy, about 1 minute. Add the sugar and beat on medium-high until mixture thickens and lightens in color, about 2 minutes. Stir in the cooled chocolate mixture, then gently fold in the dry ingredients.

▶ Pour the batter into four 1-cup ramekins or custard cups. (The batter will come almost to the rims.) Carefully place the filled ramekins in the baking pan, making sure that the water comes no higher than ⅓ of the way up the sides of the cups.

▶ Bake until the tops of soufflés are firm to the touch and slightly cracked, about 30 minutes. Gently remove the ramekins from the water and cool for 5 minutes. Dust lightly with confectioners' sugar and serve warm.

Serves 4

Baked Apples with Cinnamon-Raisin Filling

Choose large, firm apples such as Macouns, Romes, or Winesaps for baking. The apples are filled with raisins, brown sugar, and cinnamon and then basted with cider.

2	tablespoons unsalted butter, cut into small pieces
⅓	cup raisins
¼	cup firmly packed brown sugar
½	teaspoon ground cinnamon
4	large baking apples (about 2 pounds)
⅔	cup apple cider
	Whipped cream, sour cream, or vanilla ice cream, optional

▶ Preheat the oven to 375°. Combine the butter, raisins, brown sugar, and cinnamon in a small bowl, working the mixture with your fingers until the ingredients are well combined. Set the filling aside.

▶ Core the apples; then carefully remove a strip of the peel from around the stem end of each. Divide the raisin filling among the hollowed-out cores. Place the apples in a small baking dish and pour the cider into the bottom of the dish.

▶ Bake, basting the apples occasionally with some cider, until the centers can be easily pierced with a knife, 40 to 45 minutes.

▶ Serve warm with the juices from the pan. For a special treat, add some whipped cream, sour cream, or even a small scoop of vanilla ice cream.

Serves 4

"It wasn't that big a deal. It was balled up socks. And a melon."

Chandler:
And this man-child, he has no problem with how old you are?

Monica:
No, of course not. It's not even an issue. 'Cause I told him I was twenty-two.

Chandler:
What?

Monica:
What? I can't pass for twenty-two?

Phoebe:
Well, maybe twenty-five, twenty-six.

Monica:
I am twenty-six.

Phoebe:
There you go.

Ethan:
Before we get into any "staying over" stuff, there's something you should know. . . .

Monica:
Okay, is this like, "I've got an early class tomorrow," or "I'm secretly married to a goat"?

Ross:
I'm supposed to attach a brackety thing to the side things using a bunch of these little worm guys. I have no brackety things. I see no worm guys whatsoever. And I cannot feel my legs.

Strawberry Tart

Nothing could be simpler than this filling—freshly sliced strawberries tossed with warm strawberry jam, which gives them a lovely sheen. A dollop of whipped cream or even sour cream would be welcome.

Shell

2	**cups flour**
¼	**teaspoon salt**
2	**tablespoons sugar**
12	**tablespoons (1½ sticks) chilled unsalted butter**
2	**large egg yolks**

2 to 3 tablespoons ice water

Filling

2	**pints fresh strawberries**
⅓	**cup strawberry jam**
	Whipped cream or sour cream, optional but very nice

▶ Place the flour, salt, and sugar in the work bowl of a food processor and pulse until just combined. Cut the butter into small pieces and add them to the work bowl. Pulse just until the butter is cut into tiny bits. Add the yolks and pulse until well combined. Add the water 1 tablespoon at a time and pulse until the dough just comes together in a ball.

▶ Wrap the dough in plastic and refrigerate for 1 hour. Preheat the oven to 400°. Roll the dough out on a floured counter into a 12-inch circle. Fit the dough into a 10-inch tart pan with a removable bottom. Line the dough with a piece of waxed paper and weight down with dried beans or pie weights. Bake the weighted dough for 20 minutes. Remove the waxed paper and weights and reduce the heat to 350°. Continue baking until the tart shell is golden brown, about 15 minutes. (Stick close by because a burned tart shell cannot be rescued.) Cool the tart pan on a rack.

▶ When ready to serve tart, hull and slice the berries in half lengthwise and place them in a medium bowl. Heat the jam in a small saucepan set over low heat. When the jam thins out, add it to the bowl with the berries and toss gently. Arrange berries cut side down in the baked tart shell. (Make a fancy or simple pattern, depending on your artistic inclinations.) Cut the tart into wedges and serve with very lightly sweetened whipped cream (the tart is quite sweet) or even sour cream.

Serves 6 to 8

Apricot Turnovers

Frozen puff pastry (available in most supermarkets) can be turned into quick, jam-filled turnovers with very little work. Feel free to substitute other jams.

1	**sheet (about ½ pound) frozen puff pastry**
½	**cup seedless apricot preserves**
1	**large egg, beaten well**
2	**tablespoons sliced almonds**
2	**teaspoons sugar**

▶ Remove the puff pastry from freezer and thaw at room temperature for 20 minutes. Preheat the oven to 425° and lightly mist a large baking sheet with water.

▶ When the puff pastry has softened, unfold, and then roll it into a 12-inch square on a lightly floured counter. Cut the rolled puff pastry into four 6-inch squares. Place 2 tablespoons jam in the center of each square, and brush the edges with a little water. Fold the pastry over to make a triangle. Crimp edges shut with a fork.

▶ Transfer the turnovers to a large baking sheet. Brush the tops with the beaten egg, and carefully arrange some sliced almonds over the center of each turnover. Sprinkle the tops with sugar. Make three or four short slits on the top of each turnover to allow steam to escape.

▶ Bake the turnovers until puffed and golden, 12 to 14 minutes. Transfer the baking sheet to a rack. Cool for at least 15 minutes (the filling will be scorching hot unless you wait). Serve warm.

Serves 4

Quick Gingerbread

Moist gingerbread can be made while dinner is in the oven (or between commercial breaks) for a quick dessert or snack. This spiced cake really needs some whipped cream or vanilla ice cream.

6	tablespoons (¾ stick) unsalted butter, melted
½	cup firmly packed light brown sugar
½	cup molasses
1	large egg
2	cups flour
1	teaspoon baking powder
1	teaspoon baking soda
2	teaspoons ground ginger
1	teaspoon ground cinnamon
¼	teaspoon salt
½	cup milk
	Whipped cream or vanilla ice cream

▶ Preheat the oven to 350°. Grease an 8-inch-square baking pan and set it aside.

▶ Beat the melted butter, sugar, and molasses with an electric mixer for about 1 minute. Beat in the egg until smooth. Whisk the flour, baking powder, baking soda, spices, and salt together in a medium bowl. Slowly add the dry ingredients to the batter, alternating with some of the milk. Continue mixing just until all of the dry ingredients and milk have been incorporated. Pour the batter into the prepared pan.

▶ Bake the gingerbread until a toothpick inserted in the center of the cake comes out basically clean (a few crumbs are fine), about 30 minutes. Cool briefly on a rack. Serve warm with whipped cream or ice cream.

Serves 6 to 8

Rachel:
What am I going to do? What am I going to do?

Monica:
You stay here, just wait by the phone, spray Lysol in my shoe, and wait for Ross to kill you.

Rachel:
Does anybody want to trade?

Ross:
No, the vet said unless he's in a place where he has regular access to some . . . monkey lovin', he's gonna get vicious. I've got to get him into a zoo.

Joey:
How do you get a monkey into a zoo?

Chandler:
I know that one. No, that's Popes into a Volkswagen.

Monkey Lovin' Mocha Mouthfuls

When the vet says that Marcel is gonna get vicious unless he has regular access to some "monkey lovin'," Ross has no choice but to send him to a zoo. And we all know that humans, too, can get pretty testy when denied proper affection. These tiny mocha cupcakes are the best substitute when love has been lost. (At least it's better than being packed off to a zoo.)

4	**tablespoons (½ stick) unsalted butter**
2	**ounces semisweet chocolate**
⅓	**cup sugar**
I	**large egg**
I	**tablespoon coffee liqueur (such as Kahlua)**
I	**teaspoon instant espresso powder**
⅓	**cup flour**
⅓	**cup chopped walnuts, plus 12 walnut halves**

▶ Preheat the oven to 350°. Generously grease a 12-cup mini-muffin tin (the kind with cups that are about 2 inches across) and set it aside.

▶ Melt the butter and chocolate together in the top of a double boiler or in a microwave set to medium power, stirring occasionally until smooth. Set the mixture aside to cool slightly. Stir in the sugar until smooth. Whisk in the egg, coffee liqueur, and espresso powder. Gently fold in the flour and chopped walnuts.

▶ Spoon the batter into the prepared tin, filling cups about ¾ full. Place a walnut half in the center of each cup. Bake until a toothpick inserted in the center of one of the cakes comes out clean, about 20 minutes. Cool the mini-cupcakes in the muffin tin for about 5 minutes and then carefully turn them out onto a wire rack. Cool completely.

Makes 12 mini-cupcakes

Ross:
Come on, lemme see them. Show them to me. I really want to see them.

Rachel:
No, get away. Stop. I'm not showing you. Get off me.

Chandler:
You know, I've had dates like this.

Chocolate-Peanut Butter Bars

Chocolate and peanuts are natural partners, especially with a good cup of java. Despite any temptations to dig right in, allow at least 30 minutes for the glaze to set before cutting into individual bars.

12	tablespoons (1½ sticks) unsalted butter, softened
⅔	cup firmly packed light brown sugar
1	large egg
1½	teaspoons vanilla extract
½	cup smooth peanut butter
1⅓	cups flour
½	teaspoon baking powder
½	cup semisweet chocolate chips

- ▶ Preheat the oven to 350°. Grease an 8-inch-square baking pan and set it aside.

- ▶ Cream the butter and sugar with an electric mixer until light and fluffy, about 1 minute. Add the egg and vanilla and beat until smooth. Beat in ¼ cup peanut butter until smooth. Stir the flour and baking powder together. Stir the flour mixture into the batter until just combined.

- ▶ Spread the batter evenly into the prepared pan, using your fingers or a spatula. Bake until a toothpick inserted in the center of the pan comes out clean, 18 to 20 minutes. Cool the pan on a rack for 10 minutes.

- ▶ While the pan is cooling, combine the chocolate chips and remaining ¼ cup peanut butter in a small saucepan set over low heat. Stir until the chocolate

melts and the mixture is smooth.

- ▶ Spread the glaze evenly over the top of the bars. Cool for at least 30 minutes to allow the glaze to harden and set. Cut into bars.

Makes 12 bars

Absolute Best Brownies

By far, these are the best brownies in all New York, if not the world. You must use unsweetened baking chocolate. Because this bitter chocolate is inedible as is, it should be easy to keep some in the pantry. Even when the strongest chocolate craving strikes, you won't be tempted by this unsweetened stuff. As for nuts, the world is divided into two types of people: those who won't eat brownies with nuts and those who think brownies without nuts are "half-baked."

8	tablespoons (1 stick) unsalted butter
2	ounces unsweetened baking chocolate
⅔	cup flour
½	teaspoon baking powder
¼	teaspoon salt
1	cup sugar
2	large eggs
1	teaspoon vanilla extract
⅔	cup chopped nuts, if you like

- ▶ Preheat the oven to 350°. Grease an 8-inch-square baking pan and set it aside.

- ▶ Melt the butter and chocolate together in the top of a double boiler or in a microwave set to medium power, stirring occasionally until smooth. Set the mixture aside to cool slightly.

▶ Mix the flour, baking powder, and salt together in a small bowl; set the dry ingredients aside.

▶ Stir the sugar into the chocolate mixture. Beat in the eggs and vanilla by hand; then carefully fold in the flour mixture. Add nuts, if desired.

▶ Pour the batter into the prepared pan. Bake until a toothpick inserted halfway between the center and edge of the pan comes out fairly clean, 20 to 25 minutes. Cool the brownies on a rack (a half hour is the absolute minimum; an hour or two is better). Cut into squares and serve.

Makes 12 bars

Lorraine's Chocolate Mousse

When Joey and Chandler double date, Chandler usually ends up depressed (or with Janice) and Joey seems to have his way with women. One night, Joey and his date, Lorraine, decide to leave before dinner, talking about slathering and such. Chandler should be so lucky.

6   **ounces finest bittersweet or semisweet chocolate**

3   **tablespooons (½ stick) unsalted butter, softened**

2   **tablespoons orange- or coffee-flavored liqueur**

6   **large eggs, separated into yolks and whites**

½   **cup heavy cream**

¼   **cup sugar**

▶ Melt the chocolate in the top of a double boiler or in a microwave set to medium power, stirring occasionally until smooth. Stir in the butter until melted. Stir in the liqueur and set the mixture aside.

▶ Beat the egg yolks with an electric mixer until light in color, about 3 minutes. Fold in the cooled chocolate mixture. Whip the cream with an electric mixer until fluffy and soft. Fold the whipped cream into the chocolate mixture.

▶ Beat the egg whites with an electric mixer until foamy. Gradually sprinkle in the sugar and continue beating until the egg whites are stiff. Fold the egg whites into the chocolate mixture. Divide the mousse among four tall goblets and chill until ready to serve.

Serves 4

"Welcome to the real world. It sucks. You're gonna love it.**"**

Joey:
She said she wants to slather my body with stuff and lick it off me. I'm not even sure what "slathering" is, but I definitely wanna be a part of it.

Chandler:
You cannot do this to me.

Joey:
You're right. I'm sorry.

Lorraine:
Uh, can we get three chocolate mousses to go, please?

Joey:
I'm outta here. Here's my credit card. Dinner's on me. I'm sorry, Chandler.

Chandler:
I hope she throws up on you.

Joey:
Thanks.

David Schwimmer / ROSS

Among David Schwimmer's television credits are a starring role in the comedy *Monty* and recurring roles on *NYPD Blue* (as the vigilante character 4B), *Blossom*, *L.A. Law*, and *The Wonder Years*. He also starred in *A Deadly Science* and made a guest-star appearance on *Walter and Emily*. His feature film credits include *Crossing the Bridge* and *Flight of the Intruder*, as well as *Twenty Bucks* and *Wolf*. His extensive stage credits include *West, The Odyssey, Of One Blood, J.B., Rimers of Eldritch, Oh Dad, Poor Dad, Private Wars*, and *The Frog Prince*. Schwimmer was raised in Los Angeles by parents who are both attorneys. A graduate of Northwestern University, Schwimmer has also directed several plays, including *The Jungle* (which earned six Joseph Awards in Chicago), *The Serpent*, and *Alice in Wonderland*, performed at the Edinburgh Festival in Scotland.

Melanie's Fruit Salad

It would be an understatement to say that Joey has dated a lot of women. Remember Melanie, the woman who ran a fruit basket business called the Three Basketteers? If this champagne-spiked salad had been her specialty, her business might have been a success.

¾   **cup champagne or sparkling wine**

½   **cup sugar**

¾   **cup orange juice**

3   **cups honeydew melon, cut into ½-inch chunks**

3   **cups cantaloupe melon, cut into ½-inch chunks**

2   **cups red seedless grapes**

2   **cups sliced strawberries**

2   **cups blueberries**

▶ Bring the champagne and sugar to a boil in a small saucepan. Simmer, stirring frequently, just until the sugar has dissolved. Remove the pan from the heat and stir in the orange juice. Chill the mixture in the refrigerator while preparing the fruit.

▶ As you prepare each fruit, place it in a large serving bowl. When all the fruit is in the bowl, add the chilled champagne syrup. Mix gently, and spoon fruit salad into bowls. The fruit salad can be refrigerated for several hours before serving, if desired.

Serves 8 to 10

Index